ADVENT AND CHRISTMAS WITH ARCHBISHOP FULTON SHEEN

A Devotional Journey of Waiting, Welcoming, and Living the Mystery

Allan Smith

Scripture quotations in this book are taken from the Revised Standard Version – Catholic Edition, Second Edition (RSV-2CE).

Archbishop Fulton J. Sheen himself often quoted from the Douay-Rheims Bible; this edition uses the RSV-2CE for clarity while preserving the devotional tone of his insights.

Excerpts from the works of Archbishop Fulton J. Sheen are used with permission where applicable.

Quotations from Archbishop Fulton J. Sheen's published works are included for devotional use. All rights remain with their respective copyright holders.

Published by: Bishop Sheen Today

www.bishopsheentoday.com

Title: Advent and Christmas with Archbishop Fulton Sheen. A Devotional Journey of Waiting, Welcoming, and Living the Mystery

Compiled by Allan J. Smith. Includes bibliographical references.

Identifiers:

ISBN (Paperback): 978-1-997627-75-3
ISBN (eBook): 978-1-997627-76-0
ISBN (Hardcover): 978-1-997627-77-7

Subjects: Jesus Christ — Christmas – Advent - The Holy Hour — Prayer and Meditation – The Holy Face Devotion – Archbishop Fulton J. Sheen

Epiphany Edition 2026

Dedication

To Our Lady

of the Holy Name of God

&

To all who long for
Christ to be born anew
in their hearts this
Advent and Christmas

Table of Contents

PART I
The Waiting (Advent)

PART II
The Coming (Christmas)

PART III
The Living Mystery (Beyond Christmas Day)

PART IV
The Twelve Days of Christmas: The Faith Remembered

Epigraph

"The people who walked in darkness have seen a great light; those who dwelt in a land of deep darkness, on them has light shined.

For to us a child is born, to us a son is given; and the government will be upon his shoulder, and his name will be called "Wonderful Counselor, Mighty God, Everlasting Father, Prince of Peace."

Of the increase of his government and of peace there will be no end, upon the throne of David, and over his kingdom, to establish it, and to uphold it with justice and with righteousness from this time forth and for evermore. The zeal of the Lord of hosts will do this.

(Isaiah 9:2, 6,7)

"Christmas is not a day; it is a state of the soul."

— Archbishop Fulton J. Sheen
Christmas Inspirations

Editor's Note

Archbishop Fulton J. Sheen (1895–1979) was one of the most gifted Catholic preachers and teachers of the twentieth century. His Advent and Christmas reflections, especially those found in three of his books, *Christmas Inspirations (1966)*, *The World's First Love (1952)* and *Life of Christ (1958)*, continue to inspire hearts with their clarity, warmth, and depth of faith.

This present volume, *Advent and Christmas with Fulton J. Sheen*, is not a reprint of any one of Sheen's works. Rather, it is a devotional companion that draws upon his published writings, sermons, and meditations to help today's reader enter more deeply into the mysteries of the season.

Short excerpts from Sheen's writings are woven into each chapter, but they are always presented alongside new reflections, meditations, prayers, and practical applications. The aim is to let Sheen's timeless voice speak again — while also providing fresh guidance for individuals, families, and parishes who wish to live Advent and Christmas with greater devotion.

Readers are encouraged to turn not only to this little book, but also to Sheen's original works. There one will find the full treasure of his thought: the union of intellect and heart, of theology and devotion, which made him a trusted guide for millions.

It is my prayer that this devotional will allow a new generation to experience what Sheen so often proclaimed: *"Christmas is not a day, but a state of the soul — when Christ is born anew in us."*

With every blessing,
Allan J. Smith

Seasonal Reading Guide

How to Use This Book

This devotional is meant to be flexible — you may use it in several ways:

- **One or Two Chapters per Week**: Read one chapter for each week of Advent and Christmas, letting the meditations deepen gradually.

- **Daily Reflection**: Choose a Scripture passage, Sheen quote or a few reflections each day and carry it in your prayer.

- **Family Prayer**: Use the prayers, hymns, and family devotions around the crib or at the dinner table.

- **Holy Hour**: Bring this book with you before the Blessed Sacrament, using the meditations and the guide in Appendix VI.

- **Parish or Group Use**: Select one or two chapters to share in small groups or parish missions, accompanied by prayer and hymns.

Above all, let the Spirit guide you. The mystery of Advent and Christmas is not about how much we read, but about how deeply Christ is welcomed into our hearts.

PART I

The Waiting
(Advent)

CHAPTER 1

Prophecy and Promise

❧

Scripture
Isaiah 9:2, 6–7

"The people who walked in darkness have seen a great light; those who dwelt in a land of deep darkness, on them has light shined.

For to us a child is born, to us a son is given; and the government will be upon his shoulder, and his name will be called Wonderful Counselor, Mighty God, Everlasting Father, Prince of Peace. Of the increase of his government and of peace there will be no end..."

Fulton J. Sheen's Reflection

"The Old Testament is incomplete without the New, for it is like a riddle without the answer, a problem without a solution. Advent is the time when we wait for God to supply the answer. For centuries the world longed for a deliverer, and at last God Himself broke the silence. What men could not do for themselves, God did for them."

—*Christmas Inspirations*

Meditation

Advent begins with longing. Israel's prophets spoke of light in the darkness, a kingdom of peace, a child who would be both Son of David and Son of God. The waiting was centuries long, yet every promise carried a seed of hope.

3

Archbishop Sheen reminds us that human history, left to itself, is a puzzle we cannot solve. Political leaders, philosophers, and reformers have tried, but the deepest ache of the human heart remains unhealed. Only God's entry into our story could complete the unfinished riddle.

This first week of Advent, we stand with the prophets and patriarchs. Their cry is our cry: *"O come, O come, Emmanuel!"* Their darkness is our darkness: wars, divisions, personal struggles, and spiritual dryness. Yet their promise is also our promise: that God will not abandon His people.

Application

Consider what promises of God you need to hold onto this Advent. Perhaps it is His promise of peace amid anxiety, His promise of mercy for past sins, or His promise of strength in weakness. Write one of God's promises on a card and keep it with you this week as a reminder that His Word is faithful.

Prayer

**Come, Lord Jesus,
You are the Light promised by the prophets and the Hope of every heart.
Dispel the darkness of my soul with Your presence, and teach me to trust in Your promises.
May this Advent be for me a season of waiting, watching, and welcoming You anew. Amen.**

Suggested Practice

Light the first candle of the Advent wreath. As you do, read *Isaiah 9:2* aloud and pray that Christ's light may shine in your home, your parish, and in the world's darkest places.

CHAPTER 2

Mary's Fiat

❦

Scripture
Luke 1:26–31, 38

"In the sixth month the angel Gabriel was sent from God to a city of Galilee named Nazareth, to a virgin betrothed to a man whose name was Joseph, of the house of David; and the virgin's name was Mary. And he came to her and said, 'Hail, full of grace, the Lord is with you!' But she was greatly troubled at the saying, and considered in her mind what sort of greeting this might be.

And the angel said to her, 'Do not be afraid, Mary, for you have found favor with God. And behold, you will conceive in your womb and bear a son, and you shall call his name Jesus.'

… And Mary said, 'Behold, I am the handmaid of the Lord; let it be to me according to your word.' And the angel departed from her."

Fulton J. Sheen's Reflection

"Mary was not full of grace because she said *Fiat*; she said *Fiat* because she was full of grace. Grace did not come after her consent but was already in her, and it was that grace which enabled her to give her consent."

— *The World's First Love*

7

Meditation

The angel's greeting startled Mary. Heaven's announcement broke into the quiet simplicity of her hidden life in Nazareth. Yet in that moment of divine invitation, Mary responded not with hesitation but with surrender: *"Let it be done."*

Archbishop Sheen reminds us that Mary's response was not the product of sudden courage, but the fruit of a heart already filled with grace. Her whole life had been a preparation for this hour. Grace formed her, and grace carried her through.

Every Advent, we too are invited to echo Mary's *fiat*. God asks us to make room for His Word, not merely as an idea, but as a living presence that will change our lives. Like Mary, we are not asked to understand everything, but to surrender everything.

Application

Reflect today on one area of your life where God is asking for a *yes*. It may be in prayer, forgiveness, generosity, or sacrifice. What holds you back from saying, *"Be it done to me according to Your word"*? Offer that hesitation to the Lord in prayer and ask Mary to strengthen your surrender.

Prayer

Heavenly Father,

Through the "yes" of the Virgin Mary, the Word became flesh and dwelt among us. Grant me the grace to echo her surrender, to trust in Your plan even when I cannot see the whole picture.

Mary, Mother of God, pray for me, that I may say my own fiat each day. Amen.

Suggested Practice

Pray the Angelus at morning, noon, and evening this week. Each time you pray, renew your own *fiat* with Mary, inviting the Word to take flesh in your life.

CHAPTER 3

Joseph, the Silent Watchman

≈≈≈

Scripture
Matthew 1:18–21, 24

"Now the birth of Jesus Christ took place in this way. When his mother Mary had been betrothed to Joseph, before they came together, she was found to be with child of the Holy Spirit; and her husband Joseph, being a just man and unwilling to put her to shame, resolved to send her away quietly.

But as he considered this, behold, an angel of the Lord appeared to him in a dream, saying, 'Joseph, son of David, do not fear to take Mary your wife, for that which is conceived in her is of the Holy Spirit; she will bear a son, and you shall call his name Jesus, for he will save his people from their sins.' ...

When Joseph woke from sleep, he did as the angel of the Lord commanded him."

Fulton J. Sheen's Reflection

"Joseph suffered from what might be called a crucifixion of the mind. How could he reconcile Mary's great sanctity with what seemed to be evidence to the contrary? But when the angel made known the mystery, Joseph accepted his vocation as guardian of the Redeemer with a silence that speaks more than words."

— *Life of Christ*

Meditation

Joseph speaks no recorded words in Scripture. His silence is not emptiness, but attentiveness — a posture of listening before God. In the stillness of his heart, Joseph receives the divine will, not through explanation, but through trust.

Archbishop Sheen describes Joseph's trial as an interior crucifixion. To hold fast to Mary's purity while confronting what he could not yet understand demanded heroic faith. This was a suffering not of the body, but of the soul — a surrender of reason to grace. When the angel revealed the mystery, Joseph did not argue or delay; he embraced his vocation with quiet resolve.

In Joseph, we behold the guardian of both Mary and Jesus, a man whose greatness lay not in speech, but in fidelity. His witness reminds us that Advent is lived not only through words of prophecy or songs of praise, but through hearts that listen — and lives that respond in obedient love.

Application

Silence is rare in our world, but essential for hearing God's voice. Choose one day this week to practice intentional silence — perhaps turning off background noise during meals or commuting without radio or music. In that quiet, ask St. Joseph to help you discern God's will and respond with trust.

Prayer

St. Joseph, Silent guardian of the Redeemer, teach me the strength of obedience and the courage of trust. In times of confusion, give me patience; in moments of decision, give me clarity.

May I, like you, rise promptly when the Lord speaks and carry out His will with love. Amen.

Suggested Practice

Place an image or statue of St. Joseph near your Nativity scene this Advent. Each day, ask his intercession to protect your home and to guard the Christ Child who seeks to be born in your heart.

CHAPTER 4

The Expectant Soul

❧

Scripture
Romans 8:22–25

"We know that the whole creation has been groaning in travail together until now; and not only the creation, but we ourselves, who have the first fruits of the Spirit, groan inwardly as we wait for adoption as sons, the redemption of our bodies. For in this hope we were saved. Now hope that is seen is not hope. For who hopes for what he sees? But if we hope for what we do not see, we wait for it with patience."

Fulton J. Sheen's Reflection

"The Advent spirit is the spirit of vigilance. It is the call to be awake, to be expectant, to be ready for the coming of the Lord. We wait not in fear, but in joy, for the One who comes is not a tyrant but a Saviour. He comes not to destroy but to redeem."

— *Christmas Inspirations*

Meditation

All creation groans for redemption. Advent is not only a historical remembrance of Israel's longing; it is a present invitation to live with holy expectation. Archbishop Sheen reminds us that waiting is not passive but vigilant, a stance of love that keeps the lamp of faith burning in the night.

The soul that expects Christ learns to see differently. Ordinary tasks are transfigured into offerings, silence becomes a place of encounter, and even suffering becomes a preparation for glory. Just as Mary and Joseph awaited the birth of Jesus, so too every Christian soul is called to carry Christ in hiddenness until He is revealed.

Expectation is faith in action. It is trusting that God's promises are sure, even when their fulfillment seems delayed. Advent sharpens that faith, teaching us to wait with confidence, joy, and hope.

Application

This week, practice waiting with purpose. When you find yourself standing in line, driving in traffic, or holding in silence, turn that moment into prayer: "Come, Lord Jesus." In this way, every pause in your day becomes a small Advent.

Prayer

Lord Jesus,
You are the fulfillment of every longing heart.
Teach me to wait with patience, to hope with trust, and to watch with love. Let my soul be an expectant manger, ready to receive You in joy and humility. Amen.

Suggested Practice

Set aside one evening this week to keep an "Advent Holy Hour." In quiet prayer before the Blessed Sacrament — or at home near a lit candle or Nativity set — spend an hour waiting with the Lord. Offer Him your hopes, your struggles, and your longing for His coming.

PART II

The Coming
(Christmas)

CHAPTER 5

No Room at the Inn

Scripture
Luke 2:6–7

"And while they were there, the time came for her to be delivered.

And she gave birth to her first-born son and wrapped him in swaddling cloths,
and laid him in a manger, because there was no room for them in the inn."

Fulton J. Sheen's Reflection

"But when finally the scrolls of history are complete, down to the last word of time, the saddest line of all will be: *'There was no room in the inn.'*

Divinity is always where you least expect to find it. So the Son of God made man is invited to enter His own world through a back door."

— Life of Christ

Meditation

Two simple words mark the world's response to Christ at His birth: *no room.* The inns of Bethlehem were crowded with merchants, travelers, and noise. Yet the greatest Guest arrived unnoticed, pushed aside to the margins.

Archbishop Sheen reminds us that God does not storm the gates of our lives. He comes gently, seeking a place to rest. The tragedy of

Bethlehem was not deliberate cruelty but preoccupation. The innkeepers were not hostile — they were simply too busy. In their busyness, they missed the arrival of the Saviour.

How often do our own hearts resemble the crowded inn? We fill our days with schedules, distractions, anxieties, and noise — leaving little space for God. Advent culminates in this question: when Christ comes, will He find room? Or will He once again be pushed to the edges, waiting in the silence of a stable?

Application

Take time this week to "clear the inn" of your heart. Ask yourself: What noise, what clutter, what distractions keep Christ outside? Choose one unnecessary thing to set aside this week — whether an hour of screen time, a habit of rushing, or a small indulgence — and offer that space to the Lord as an open room for His presence.

Prayer

Lord Jesus,
Forgive me for the times I have closed the door to You.
Like the innkeepers of Bethlehem, I have often been too busy or distracted to recognize Your coming.
Open my eyes, widen my heart, and give me the grace to welcome You without delay.
Come, Lord Jesus, and be at home in me.

Amen.

Suggested Practice

Place a small sign or card near your Nativity scene that reads: *"Room for Christ."* Let it remind you daily that your heart, your home, and your family are meant to be a dwelling place for Him.

CHAPTER 6

The Wood of the Manger and the Cross

Scripture
Philippians 2:6–8

"Though he was in the form of God, he did not count equality with God a thing to be grasped, but emptied himself, taking the form of a servant, being born in the likeness of men.

And being found in human form he humbled himself and became obedient unto death, even death on a cross."

Fulton J. Sheen's Reflection

"The manger and the Cross are of the same wood. The crib and the Cross are but two points along the same line: one begins the story of love, the other consummates it. He accepted the cradle because He was willing to accept the Cross."

— *Life of Christ*

Meditation

The Nativity is radiant with joy but woven through its brightness is a quiet shadow. The child lying in a manger is already the Lamb destined for sacrifice. The poverty of Bethlehem foreshadows the poverty of Calvary. The wooden crib points forward to the wooden Cross.

Archbishop Sheen reminds us that Christmas cannot be separated from Good Friday. The Incarnation is not merely God entering history to share our joys; it is God entering flesh to bear our sorrows. The Word became flesh not only to dwell among us but to die for us.

At Christmas, we see love's beginning: a God who humbles Himself to share our weakness. At the Cross, we see love's fullness: a God who surrenders Himself to save us. Both manger and Cross tell the same story — love poured out, love made visible, love victorious.

Application

When you gaze at a Nativity scene this week, notice the wood of the manger. Imagine the shadow of the Cross falling across it. Let this reminder help you see your own joys and sorrows in a new light. Whatever suffering you carry, unite it to the Child who came to transform every cradle of pain into a path of redemption.

Prayer

Lord Jesus,
From the manger to the Cross, You embraced the poverty of our humanity.
Teach me to see that in every joy and every sorrow, You are present.
Give me the grace to embrace my daily crosses with love, and to walk with You from Bethlehem to Calvary, trusting that every sacrifice leads to resurrection.
Amen.

Suggested Practice

Place a small cross near your Nativity scene during this week of Christmas. Let it remind you that the Child in the crib and the Savior on the Cross are one and the same — and that His love spans the whole journey of your life.

CHAPTER 7

The Shepherds and the Magi

Scripture
Luke 2:15–16; Matthew 2:1–2, 10–11

"When the angels went away from them into heaven, the shepherds said to one another, 'Let us go over to Bethlehem and see this thing that has happened, which the Lord has made known to us.' And they went with haste, and found Mary and Joseph, and the baby lying in a manger."

"Now when Jesus was born in Bethlehem of Judea in the days of Herod the king, behold, wise men from the East came to Jerusalem, saying, 'Where is he who has been born king of the Jews? For we have seen his star in the East, and have come to worship him.' … When they saw the star, they rejoiced exceedingly with great joy; and going into the house they saw the child with Mary his mother, and they fell down and worshiped him. Then, opening their treasures, they offered him gifts of gold and frankincense and myrrh."

Fulton J. Sheen's Reflection

"The shepherds heard because they were simple. The great ones of the earth did not hear because they were too wrapped up in themselves. Later, the Magi came — the intellectuals, the seekers of wisdom. Both the simple and the learned knelt before the same Child. That is why Christ is the desire of the everlasting hills: He draws all men to Himself."

— Christmas Inspirations

Meditation

The first to come were shepherds — poor, unrefined, yet attentive to the voice of heaven. The second were Magi — wealthy, educated, guided by a star. One group was led by angels, the other by reason and science. Both found the same destination: the Christ Child in Bethlehem.

Archbishop Sheen reminds us that Christ gathers all of humanity. He is the Savior not of one class, nation, or culture, but of all who seek truth. The shepherds teach us humility and eagerness; the Magi teach us perseverance and adoration. Together they show that every path — simplicity or scholarship, poverty or wealth — finds its completion in worship.

The gifts of the Magi reveal the destiny of the Child: gold for His kingship, incense for His priesthood, and myrrh for His death. Even at the cradle, the Cross casts its shadow. Joy and sacrifice are woven together in the mystery of Christ's coming.

Application

Reflect this week on how you approach Christ. Do you come like the shepherds, in poverty of spirit and simplicity of heart? Or like the Magi, seeking truth through study, reason, and persistence? Both are welcomed. Ask the Lord to purify your worship so that, whatever path you walk, you arrive at His feet in adoration.

Prayer

Lord Jesus, You are the King of Kings and the Shepherd of souls. Receive the poverty of my heart and the treasures of my life. Teach me to bow in humility like the shepherds, and to offer my best like the Magi. May all that I am and all that I have be laid before You in love. Amen.

Suggested Practice

Place three small objects (a coin, a candle, and a small piece of spice or herb) near your Nativity scene this week. Let them remind you of the Magi's gifts — gold, frankincense, and myrrh — and offer them spiritually as your own prayer of adoration.

CHAPTER 8

The Word Made Flesh

❧

Scripture
John 1:1, 14

"In the beginning was the Word, and the Word was with God, and the Word was God... And the Word became flesh and dwelt among us, full of grace and truth; we have beheld his glory, glory as of the only Son from the Father."

Fulton J. Sheen's Reflection

"The Incarnation is the supreme meeting of opposites: eternity and time, divinity and humanity, majesty and humility. He who created the universe was wrapped in swaddling clothes; He who made the sun and stars lay beneath their light. This is the scandal of Christmas — that the infinite God became an infant."

— Life of Christ

Meditation

At Bethlehem, the eternal stepped into time. The Creator entered His creation. The invisible God became visible in the fragile body of a child. No philosophy or religion could have imagined such a union: that God would stoop so low, not only to dwell with humanity but to become one of us.

Archbishop Sheen reminds us that the Incarnation is not a temporary disguise or a passing gesture of pity. The Word became flesh permanently. Christ took on our humanity in order to redeem it, to sanctify it, and to raise it to glory.

The mystery of Christmas is not merely that God *visited* us, but that He *dwells* with us. He is Emmanuel — God with us, here and now. This is the truth that gives meaning to every joy and every sorrow: we are never alone, for the Word has pitched His tent among us.

Application

Take a few quiet minutes this week to reflect on the humanity of Christ. Imagine Him as a child — breathing, crying, reaching out for Mary and Joseph. Let this truth sink in: the God of the universe chose to become small, so that you might draw near without fear.

Prayer

Eternal Word, You became flesh and dwelt among us.
In humility You entered our world, in love You remain with us always.

Open my heart to adore You, not as a distant God, but as Emmanuel — God with me, here and now.

Amen.

Suggested Practice

Each day this week, pray slowly the words of the Creed: *"For us men and for our salvation He came down from heaven, and by the Holy Spirit was incarnate of the Virgin Mary, and became man."* Make a simple bow at these words, as the Church invites us to do, and let this gesture renew your awe at the mystery of the Incarnation.

PART III

The Living Mystery
(Beyond Christmas Day)

CHAPTER 9

The Birth of Christ in the Soul

❧

Scripture
Galatians 4:4–6

"But when the fullness of time had come, God sent forth his Son, born of woman, born under the law, to redeem those who were under the law, so that we might receive adoption as sons. And because you are sons, God has sent the Spirit of his Son into our hearts, crying, 'Abba! Father!'"

Fulton J. Sheen's Reflection

"There are two births of Christ, one unto the world in Bethlehem; the other in the soul, when it is spiritually reborn. It was the second birth that St. Paul insisted on when he said: 'Until Christ be formed in you.' What good would it be if Christ were born a thousand times in Bethlehem, if He is not born in our hearts?"

— *Christmas Inspirations*

Meditation

Bethlehem happened once in history, but it must happen again in every soul. The Incarnation is not just a past event to admire; it is a living mystery to be received.

Archbishop Sheen teaches that the stable of Bethlehem becomes the sanctuary of our hearts when Christ dwells within us. Just as Mary offered her body to become His dwelling place, so too we are called to offer our lives as His home. Each act of faith, each surrender to grace, is another "yes" to the Word who desires to be born within us.

Christmas joy deepens when we realize that Christ is not only *with us* but *in us*. His presence transforms us into living mangers, carrying His light into a darkened world. The true miracle of Christmas is not only that God became man, but that He still chooses to be born in every believer who welcomes Him.

Application

Ask yourself: *Have I welcomed Christ into the inn of my soul, or is He still waiting outside?* This week, prepare a place for Him by making a sincere confession, renewing your baptismal promises, or setting aside extra time for prayer. Let your soul become a Bethlehem where Christ is born anew.

Prayer

Lord Jesus,

You were born in Bethlehem to be born again in me. Come into the stable of my soul, humble though it is, and make it Your dwelling place.

Form in me a new heart, filled with Your Spirit, that I may carry Your light to others. Amen.

Suggested Practice

Place a small piece of straw, hay, or a strip of cloth in your Nativity scene to represent your own heart. Each day, as you see it, pray: *"Lord, be born in me today."*

CHAPTER 10

The Child and the Cross

❧

Scripture
Luke 2:34–35

"And Simeon blessed them and said to Mary his mother,

'Behold, this child is set for the fall and rising of many in Israel, and for a sign that is spoken against— and a sword will pierce through your own soul also — that thoughts out of many hearts may be revealed.'"

Fulton J. Sheen's Reflection

"The shadow of the Cross fell across Bethlehem. The Christ Child is not to be separated from the Man of Sorrows. He accepted the cradle because He was willing to accept the Cross. In His birth was written His death; in His coming was contained His sacrifice."

— Life of Christ

Meditation

The arms that reached for His mother in Bethlehem would one day stretch wide upon the Cross. The wood of the manger foreshadows the wood of Calvary. Even in the joy of Christmas, there is a quiet gravity: this Child was born to die.

Archbishop Sheen insists that we cannot understand Christmas apart from Good Friday. The Incarnation was not God's sentimental gesture but His saving mission. Love compelled Him not only to share our life but to give His life. The swaddling clothes of Bethlehem prefigure the burial cloths of the tomb.

For Mary, Simeon's prophecy was both a blessing and a wound. She would cradle her Son in her arms at Bethlehem and again at Calvary. The sword that pierced her soul is the reminder that divine love is always costly. To love Christ is to follow Him to the Cross.

Application

Reflect this week on how the Cross is present in your life. What suffering, trial, or sacrifice has God allowed you to bear? Instead of resisting it, place it at the manger. Say to the Child: *"I accept this cross because You accepted Yours."* In doing so, you unite your pain to His redeeming love.

Prayer

Lord Jesus,
From the cradle to the Cross, You embraced the path of sacrifice.
Teach me to carry my daily crosses with patience and love.
May I never separate the joy of Your birth from the mystery of Your
Passion, but see in both the fullness of Your love for me.

Amen.

Suggested Practice

During the Christmas season, place a small cross near your Nativity scene. Each time you pass it, pray: *"Lord Jesus, may my life be united to Yours, from Bethlehem to Calvary."*

CHAPTER 11

The Family of Nazareth

Scripture
Luke 2:51–52

"And he went down with them and came to Nazareth, and was obedient to them; and his mother kept all these things in her heart. And Jesus increased in wisdom and in stature, and in favor with God and man."

Fulton J. Sheen's Reflection

"The modern family is crumbling because it has forgotten Nazareth. God Himself chose to enter into a family, to be subject to parents, to sanctify the home. The recovery of family life begins not with social programs, but with a crib in which Christ is honored, a Mother who loves, and a father who provides and protects."

— *The World's First Love*

Meditation

For thirty years, the Son of God lived in obscurity at Nazareth. No miracles, no public teaching, no great works — only the daily rhythm of home: meals shared, prayers offered, work done faithfully. By living in a family, Christ revealed the holiness of ordinary life.

Archbishop Sheen reminds us that the Holy Family is not a distant ideal but a living model. Mary embodies love and faith, Joseph embodies fidelity and strength, and Christ embodies obedience and growth. In their unity, we glimpse God's plan for every household: a school of love, sacrifice, and holiness.

In a world that often undermines family life, Nazareth stands as a beacon. The path to sainthood is not found only in cathedrals or missions, but around the dinner table, in shared work, and in patient forgiveness within the home.

Application

Reflect on your own family life — whether as spouse, parent, child, or spiritual member of God's household. How can you bring the spirit of Nazareth into your home? Choose one simple act this week: pray together as a family, share a meal without distractions, or speak a word of encouragement where there has been tension.

Prayer

Jesus, Mary, and Joseph, Holy Family of Nazareth, be the model for our homes.
Teach us love, fidelity, and sacrifice.
Sanctify the ordinary duties of our daily lives, that we may grow in wisdom and favor with God and man.

Amen.

Suggested Practice

Place a small image of the Holy Family in a central place in your home during the Christmas season. Each day, ask their intercession for peace, unity, and holiness in your family.

CHAPTER 12

Advent and Christmas as a Way of Life

~~~~~~~~~

Scripture
John 1:16–17

"From his fullness we have all received, grace upon grace.

For the law was given through Moses;
grace and truth came through Jesus Christ."

Fulton J. Sheen's Reflection

"Christmas is not a day, it is a state of the soul. The crib, the Cross, and the altar are one and the same mystery of divine love. If Christ is born in us daily, then every day is Christmas, and every sacrifice becomes a sharing in His redemptive love."

— *Christmas Inspirations*

Meditation

The Church gives us four weeks of Advent and twelve days of Christmas, but the mystery is meant to extend far beyond the calendar. Advent teaches us to wait with hope; Christmas teaches us to welcome with joy — and both call us to live with Christ every day.

Archbishop Sheen insists that Christmas is not just a sentimental celebration but a continual reality: Christ dwelling in us, grace upon grace. The same Christ who came to Bethlehem now comes in the Eucharist. The same Christ who was laid in a manger now rests within our souls.

To live Advent and Christmas as a way of life is to see every moment as expectant, every encounter as holy, every sacrifice as redemptive. The waiting never ends, because we await His final coming in glory. The joy never ends, because He is already Emmanuel — God with us.

Application

As this season draws to a close, ask yourself: how will I keep the light of Christmas burning in my daily life? Choose one practice to carry into the new year — perhaps weekly adoration, family prayer, acts of charity, or Scripture meditation. Let this be your way of living Advent watchfulness and Christmas joy all year long.

Prayer

Lord Jesus,
You are the Eternal Word who became flesh,
the Child of Bethlehem and the Savior of the world.
Grant me the grace to live always in the spirit of Advent and
Christmas — waiting with hope, welcoming with joy,
and carrying Your presence into the world each day.
Come, Lord Jesus, now and forever.

Amen.

Suggested Practice

As you put away your Nativity scene at the end of the Christmas season, keep one small piece — perhaps the figure of the Child — in a visible place all year. Let it remind you that Christmas is not over but continues in every moment you welcome Christ into your life.

PART IV

The Twelve Days of Christmas: The Faith Remembered

INTRODUCTION

A Song That
Taught the Faith

Nearly everyone knows the song *The Twelve Days of Christmas*. Few know that it once taught the faith.

What many hear today as a playful counting carol was, for generations of Christians, a quiet catechism set to music. Long before printed books were common, and during periods when open instruction in the faith was restricted or difficult, the Church found a way to teach doctrine through memory and melody.

Truth was sung before it was studied.

Each verse of the song concealed a central teaching of the Christian faith — Christ Himself, Sacred Scripture, the virtues, the Commandments, the Beatitudes, the Apostles, and the very structure of belief. What sounded like poetry was, in fact, theology remembered by the heart.

This should not surprise us. God Himself chose song as a vessel for truth. The Psalms taught Israel to pray. Mary sang the Magnificat to proclaim salvation. Angels announced Christmas not with arguments, but with music. When truth is sung, it takes root more deeply than when it is merely heard.

The Church once trusted that what was repeated joyfully would be remembered faithfully.

These reflections seek to recover that forgotten depth. They do not replace the song; they *unveil it*. Each day of Christmas is paired with its traditional meaning, explored not as a lesson to be memorized, but as a mystery to be lived.

The familiar melody remains. But now, the meaning is restored.

May these reflections help us hear the song again — not merely with nostalgia, but with understanding — and may the joy of Christmas lead us, once more, into the fullness of the faith it was meant to teach.

DAY 1

The Partridge in the Pear Tree — Christ at the Center

The carol begins not with abundance, but with *one* gift.

A single partridge, resting in a pear tree, is an image easily overlooked — yet it conceals the entire Christian faith. The partridge represents Christ Himself, and the tree upon which it rests foreshadows the Cross. Christmas, from its very first note, points beyond the crib to Calvary.

Christianity does not begin with many truths, but with one Truth made Flesh.

The partridge is known for one remarkable trait: it will feign injury to draw predators away from its young. In this, the image becomes unmistakable. Christ did not come to save from a distance. He exposed Himself to danger so that His children might live.

The pear tree reminds us that redemption grows from obedience. Where the first tree in Eden brought death through disobedience, this new tree bears life through surrender. Christmas already contains the seed of the Cross — not as tragedy, but as love's fulfillment.

The Church once taught this truth not through textbooks, but through song. Long before children could articulate Christology, they could sing it. And in singing, they learned that everything in the Christian life begins — and ends — with Christ.

If Christmas is reduced to sentiment, it fades quickly. If it is centered on Christ, it endures.

Remove the partridge, and the song collapses. Remove Christ, and faith becomes noise.

Prayer

Lord Jesus Christ,
Partridge who gave Yourself to save Your young,
teach me to place You at the center of all things.
Let my faith begin and end with You,
my choices be measured by You,
and my love be shaped by Your sacrifice.

Strip away what distracts me from Your Cross,
and anchor my life in the one Truth made Flesh,
that everything I believe, hope, and love
may rest securely in You.

Amen.

Christianity begins not with many gifts, but with one
— Christ Himself, offered for the life of the world.

DAY 2

The Two Turtle Doves
— The Word Given Twice

Christmas does not leave us guessing about God.

The carol speaks of *two turtle doves* — gentle, faithful, inseparable. Hidden beneath the poetry is one of the Church's most enduring truths: God has spoken to man *twice* — once in preparation, and once in fulfillment. The two turtle doves represent the **Old and New Testaments**, bound together by a single divine Author.

God did not contradict Himself when Christ came; He completed Himself.

The Old Testament is not a discarded beginning, but a promise patiently unfolding. The New Testament is not a replacement, but a revelation. What was hinted at in shadow becomes visible in light. What was foretold in prophecy stands fulfilled in a Person.

The tragedy of modern Christianity is not disbelief, but *selective belief*.

Some wish for the comfort of the New Testament without the demands of the Old. Others cling to law without embracing love. The two turtle doves remind us that truth is never divided against itself. Mercy does not abolish justice; it crowns it. Love does not erase the law; it perfects it.

Scripture is a conversation between God and man — and Christ is the answer spoken aloud.

In the Old Testament, God promises a Savior.
In the New Testament, He sends Him.

In the Old, Christ is anticipated.
In the New, He is encountered.

Christmas stands precisely at this meeting point.

The Child in the manger is the living bridge between covenant and fulfillment. Every prophecy bends toward Him. Every promise rests upon Him. To separate Christ from Scripture is to silence God's voice. To read Scripture without Christ is to miss its meaning.

The Church once taught this unity through song because unity must be remembered before it can be defended. Long before theology was argued, it was sung — and thus carried safely through generations.

The two turtle doves do not fly apart. Neither should the Christian who wishes to understand Christ.

Prayer

Lord Jesus,
Word made Flesh,
open my heart to receive the fullness of Your truth.
Teach me to love all that You have revealed,
to hear Your voice in all of Scripture,
and to live according to the Word
that leads to eternal life.
Amen.

God spoke twice so that man would not misunderstand Him
— once in promise, and once in fulfillment.

DAY 3

The Three French Hens
— Faith, Hope, and Charity

Christianity is not sustained by ideas alone.
It lives by virtue.

The carol gives us *three French hens* — a curious image, easily dismissed — yet beneath it lies the very structure of the Christian soul. These three gifts represent the **theological virtues: Faith, Hope, and Charity** — infused by God, oriented toward God, and completed in God.

They are called *theological* not because they are lofty, but because they cannot be manufactured. No one reasons his way into faith, wills himself into hope, or practices his way into charity. These virtues are received before they are exercised.

Grace always precedes effort.

Faith allows us to believe in God.
Hope allows us to trust in His promises.
Charity allows us to love as He loves.

Remove any one of these, and the Christian life collapses. Faith without hope becomes fear. Hope without charity becomes self-interest. Charity without faith becomes sentiment. Together, they form a living harmony — not unlike a song repeated day after day, growing stronger through repetition.

Christmas gives us the reason these virtues are possible.

Faith believes because God has spoken.
Hope endures because God has come.
Charity loves because God has given Himself.

The Child in the manger is the proof that faith is reasonable, hope is justified, and love is demanding. Christmas is not merely the reassurance that God exists, but the revelation that He *cares enough to enter our condition.*

The modern world often replaces these virtues with substitutes. Opinion takes the place of faith. Optimism replaces hope. Tolerance stands in for charity. But substitutes cannot sustain the soul. Only what comes from God can lead back to God.

The Church once taught this through song because virtue must be learned early — before skepticism hardens the heart. Children sang what saints would later live.

If Christmas is to survive beyond the season, it must take root in these three virtues. Decorations fade. Music quiets. But faith believes still. Hope waits still. Charity loves still.

And where these three abide, Christ remains.

Prayer

Lord Jesus, born to awaken faith,
to anchor hope, and to ignite charity,
strengthen these virtues within my soul.
May I believe more firmly, hope more confidently,
and love more generously, for love of You. Amen.

Faith believes because God has spoken, hope endures because God has come, and charity loves because God has given Himself.

DAY 4

The Four Calling Birds
— The Gospel Proclaimed

Truth was never meant to whisper.

The carol speaks of *four calling birds* — not silent, not hidden, but calling. Their song represents the **Four Gospels**: Matthew, Mark, Luke, and John — four distinct voices united in one proclamation: *Jesus Christ is Lord.*

God did not entrust the Good News to a single voice, but to four, so that no one could mistake its meaning.

Each Gospel calls from a different height, yet all call toward the same truth. Matthew speaks to the heart of Israel, revealing Christ as the promised Messiah. Mark moves swiftly, proclaiming Christ in action and authority. Luke writes with compassion, presenting the Savior of the poor and the outcast. John soars, unveiling the eternal Word made Flesh.

Different voices. One message.

The four calling birds remind us that the Gospel is not invented; it is announced. Christianity is not a private insight, but a public proclamation. The Good News demands to be spoken aloud — not merely admired in silence.

Modern man often wishes for a Gospel that adapts itself to the world. The Church proclaims a Gospel that calls the world to conversion.

The Gospels do not flatter human pride; they summon human freedom. They call us out of sin, out of complacency, and out of silence. To hear the Gospel is to be addressed personally. To ignore it is to refuse the call.

Christmas itself is a proclamation. The angels announced it. The shepherds repeated it. The Church continues it. From the crib onward, Christ is meant to be spoken of, shared, and proclaimed.

The four calling birds do not sing four different songs. They sing one harmony — the Word made Flesh, crucified and risen, calling every generation to respond.

Prayer

Lord Jesus,
living Word of the Father,
open my heart to hear Your Gospel
and give me courage to respond to its call.
May I never silence the truth through fear or comfort,
but proclaim by my life
what the Church proclaims with her voice.
Amen.

The Gospel was never meant to be admired in silence,
but proclaimed with conviction.

DAY 5

The Five Golden Rings — The Law That Leads to Love

Gold is precious because it endures.

The carol gives us *five golden rings* — radiant, unbroken, and enduring — symbolizing the **first five books of the Bible**, the Law given to Israel: Genesis, Exodus, Leviticus, Numbers, and Deuteronomy. These books are not relics of a forgotten age; they are the golden foundation upon which the Gospel stands.

God did not begin salvation with grace alone. He began with truth.

The Law was not given to imprison man, but to prepare him. It taught a wandering people who God was, who they were, and how to live in covenant. Before God revealed His mercy fully, He revealed His holiness. Before He offered forgiveness, He taught responsibility.

The Law is a mirror before it is a guide.

Modern man resists law because he mistakes it for limitation. Yet the absence of law does not produce freedom; it produces confusion. Just as rings have no beginning or end, the moral law reflects the eternal wisdom of God — not imposed arbitrarily, but woven into creation itself.

Christ did not come to shatter these golden rings. He came to place them on the heart.

When Jesus fulfilled the Law, He did not discard it; He completed it. What was written on stone, He engraved in love. The commandments that once restrained sin became, in Christ, pathways to holiness.

Christmas reminds us that law and love are not enemies.

The Child born under the Law would one day raise humanity above it — not by abolishing obedience, but by perfecting it through grace. The five golden rings shimmer beneath the melody because they hold the song together. Remove them, and harmony collapses.

The Church once taught this truth through song because law must be loved before it can be lived. And love, when rooted in truth, becomes freedom.

Prayer

Lord Jesus,
born under the Law to redeem us,
write Your truth upon my heart.
Free me from the illusion that freedom means license,
and teach me the obedience that leads to love.
May Your commandments become my joy,
and Your truth my guide.
Amen.

The Law was given not to crush the heart,
but to prepare it for love.

DAY 6

The Six Geese a-Laying — Creation Awaiting Its Creator

Life begins with God's command — and it unfolds in order.

The carol offers *six geese a-laying*, a symbol easily overlooked, yet rich with meaning. These six gifts represent the **six days of Creation**, when God spoke the universe into being — light and land, sea and sky, plant and creature — each ordered, purposeful, and declared good.

Creation was not an accident. It was an intention.

Before there was redemption, there was design. Before grace restored the world, wisdom structured it. The six days of Creation teach us that the universe is not chaos governed by chance, but a cosmos shaped by intelligence and love. Every created thing bears the imprint of a Creator who delights in order.

Yet Creation, though good, was unfinished.

It awaited a final touch — not another command, but a Presence. At Christmas, the Creator entered His own creation. The Word through whom all things were made took flesh and dwelt among His works. The hands that shaped the stars were wrapped in swaddling clothes.

Bethlehem completes Genesis.

The world that had been made through Christ was now redeemed by Christ. Matter, once formed by His Word, was now sanctified by

His Body. Creation no longer pointed only upward; it welcomed God within.

Modern man often treats the world as something to exploit or escape. Christmas offers a different vision: creation is to be received with gratitude and offered back in praise. When Christ enters the world, the world regains its meaning.

The six days of Creation culminated in rest. Christmas begins the restoration of that rest — not as inactivity, but as harmony between God and man.

The geese lay eggs — signs of life yet to emerge. So too Creation, groaning under sin, awaited the life that would burst forth in Christ. Christmas is the dawn of a new creation, where what was broken begins to be healed.

Prayer

Lord Jesus,
through whom all things were made,
teach me to reverence Your creation.
Free me from misuse and indifference,
and help me to see the world as You see it,
a gift to be received and redeemed.
May my life reflect the harmony
You came to restore.
Amen.

The Creator entered His creation so that
creation might finally find its rest in Him.

DAY 7

The Seven Swans a-Swimming — Life Moved by the Spirit

Life does not advance by force alone.
It advances by *grace*.

The carol presents *seven swans a-swimming* — graceful, powerful, and purposeful. Beneath the image lies a profound truth of Christian life: the **Seven Gifts of the Holy Spirit**, given not to decorate the soul, but to move it forward in God's will.

The Christian life is not meant to be static.

A swan does not fight the current by frantic motion; it glides by surrendering to it. So too the soul guided by the Holy Spirit does not rely on raw effort alone, but on cooperation with divine life. Grace does not replace nature — it elevates it.

The Seven Gifts — **Wisdom, Understanding, Counsel, Fortitude, Knowledge, Piety, and Fear of the Lord** — are not medals earned by the holy, but powers infused for the weak. They complete the virtues by making us responsive to God's promptings.

Without the Spirit, faith becomes rigid.
Hope becomes fragile.
Charity becomes exhausting.

Christmas prepares us for Pentecost.

The Child born in Bethlehem comes not only to save us from sin, but to *live His own life within us*. That life flows through the Spirit. The manger points toward the Upper Room. The Infant who breathes His first breath in Bethlehem will one day breathe His Spirit upon the Church.

Modern man often believes holiness is achieved by intensity alone. The Gospel teaches otherwise. True holiness is docility — the ability to be moved by God. The Spirit leads not by shouting, but by drawing.

The seven swans swim together, not apart. The gifts of the Spirit are not isolated talents; they form a harmony. Wisdom directs understanding. Counsel guides fortitude. Fear of the Lord anchors them all in humility.

Where the Spirit is welcomed, the Christian life becomes fluid, joyful, and purposeful.

Christmas does not end with admiration of Christ. It prepares us for transformation by His Spirit.

Prayer

Holy Spirit,
Gift of the Father and the Son,
move my soul as You will.
Free me from resistance and fear,
and grant me the docility
that allows grace to carry me forward.
May Your gifts shape my thoughts,
my choices, and my love.
Amen.

Holiness is not achieved by force of will alone,
but by a soul willing to be moved by God.

DAY 8

The Eight Maids a-Milking — The Joy of the Beatitudes

Holiness does not begin with power.
It begins with emptiness.

The carol offers *eight maids a-milking* — humble, unseen laborers whose work nourishes others. Hidden within this image are the **Eight Beatitudes**, Christ's charter for Christian living and the heart of His Sermon on the Mount.

The Beatitudes do not describe the successful; they describe the blessed.

"Blessed are the poor in spirit."
"Blessed are the meek."
"Blessed are those who mourn."
"Blessed are those who hunger and thirst for righteousness."
"Blessed are the merciful."
"Blessed are the pure of heart."
"Blessed are the peacemakers."
"Blessed are those persecuted for righteousness' sake."

Each Beatitude overturns the world's definition of happiness. The world says happiness comes from possession, power, pleasure, and praise. Christ says happiness comes from surrender, humility, mercy, and truth. Christmas already teaches this lesson in silence. The Beatitudes proclaim it aloud.

Milk is nourishment given freely — not hoarded, not displayed, but poured out.

65

So too the Beatitudes nourish the soul by teaching us how to live for others rather than ourselves. They are not ideals reserved for saints; they are invitations extended to all who wish to follow Christ closely.

The modern world often reads the Beatitudes as poetry. Christ meant them as *instruction*.

The maids labor daily, faithfully, without applause. In the same way, the Beatitudes are lived quietly — in patience under insult, mercy in misunderstanding, purity in temptation, and peace in conflict. This hidden holiness is the strength of the Church.

Christmas shows us a God who chose humility. The Beatitudes show us how to respond.

They teach us that joy is not the absence of suffering, but the presence of God within it. When lived faithfully, the Beatitudes transform ordinary life into a school of holiness — one humble act at a time.

Prayer

Lord Jesus, Teacher of true happiness,
write the Beatitudes upon my heart.
Free me from false visions of success,
and teach me the joy that comes
from humility, mercy, and peace.
May my life nourish others
through quiet fidelity to Your Gospel.
Amen.

> *The world promises happiness by giving more;*
> *Christ gives happiness by asking more of the heart.*

DAY 9

The Nine Ladies Dancing — Joy Made Visible

Grace is never meant to remain hidden.

The carol presents *nine ladies dancing* — graceful, expressive, and joyful. Beneath the movement lies a profound truth: the **Nine Fruits of the Holy Spirit**, the outward signs that grace is alive and active within the soul.

Virtue is formed quietly.

Fruit is seen publicly.

St. Paul names these fruits: **charity, joy, peace, patience, kindness, goodness, faithfulness, gentleness, and self-control.** They are not talents to be displayed, but effects to be noticed. No one produces them by effort alone; they appear when the soul cooperates with grace.

A fruit tree does not strain to bear fruit. It remains rooted.

So too the Christian life bears fruit not by striving for holiness as an achievement, but by remaining united to Christ. The Fruits of the Spirit are not proof of success; they are evidence of presence — the presence of God dwelling within.

The ladies dance because joy must move. When the Spirit is alive in the soul, faith is no longer heavy, morality no longer bitter, and sacrifice no longer sterile. Even suffering, when united to Christ, takes on a mysterious rhythm of hope.

The modern world often seeks results without roots.

It wants peace without truth, joy without sacrifice, and love without commitment. The Fruits of the Spirit expose this illusion. They grow only where Christ is welcomed, His commandments respected, and His grace allowed to shape daily life.

Christmas itself is a fruit.

The Incarnation produces visible change — shepherds rejoice, Magi worship, hearts are converted, and lives redirected. When Christ truly enters a soul, others can tell. Faith becomes attractive because it becomes *alive*.

If the Beatitudes describe the road, the Fruits of the Spirit reveal the destination.

They are the quiet confirmation that God is at work — not just in the Church, but in you.

Prayer

Holy Spirit,
living source of joy and peace,
bear Your fruits within my soul.
Let my life reflect the quiet evidence
of Your presence through patience, kindness, and love.
May others encounter Christ
through the joy You awaken in me.
Amen.

Grace is known not by what it claims,
but by the fruit it quietly produces.

DAY 10

The Ten Lords a-Leaping — Freedom That Obeys

Freedom does not begin by breaking rules.
It begins by knowing the truth.

The carol speaks of *ten lords a-leaping* — strong, ordered, energetic. Beneath the image stand the **Ten Commandments**, the moral law given by God not to restrain man, but to protect him.

God did not give the commandments to slaves, but to the free.

Israel received the Law *after* liberation from Egypt, not before. The commandments were not chains, but guardrails — meant to preserve the freedom God had already bestowed. True liberty is not the ability to do whatever one wishes; it is the power to do what one ought.

The modern world fears commandments because it equates law with oppression. Yet where law is absent, the strong dominate the weak, desire replaces reason, and chaos masquerades as choice. The Ten Commandments stand as a defense of human dignity.

They protect:

- worship from idolatry

- love from exploitation

- truth from deception

- life from violence

- freedom from slavery to sin

Christ did not abolish the commandments; He *leapt* them to a higher plane.

What was once written externally, He fulfilled internally. He taught that obedience begins not with actions alone, but with the heart. Christmas prepares us for this truth by revealing a God who enters our condition, not to excuse sin, but to heal it.

The ten lords leap because moral life is meant to be dynamic.

Obedience is not stagnation. It is movement toward holiness. When the commandments are lived in love, they do not crush joy; they preserve it. They allow the soul to move freely within the harmony God intended.

Christmas reminds us that God came close enough to teach us how to live — not merely how to feel.

Prayer

Lord Jesus,
giver and fulfiller of the Law,
teach me the obedience that leads to freedom.
Free me from the illusion
that happiness comes from doing as I please,
and guide me into the joy
that comes from living in Your truth.
Amen.

The commandments do not limit freedom;
they protect it from destroying itself.

DAY 11

The Eleven Pipers Piping — Fidelity When One Falls Away

Truth does not depend on numbers.
It depends on faithfulness.

The carol gives us *eleven pipers piping* — not twelve. One is missing. Hidden within this absence is a sober lesson: the **Eleven Faithful Apostles**, who remained after one betrayed the Lord.

Christianity was born not among the perfect, but among the faithful.

Judas had walked with Christ, heard His words, witnessed His miracles — yet he chose another path. His departure did not undo the truth, nor did it invalidate the mission. The Church did not collapse because one fell away; it endured because the others remained.

This is a hard lesson for every age.

Scandal shakes faith not because it is new, but because it wounds trust. Yet Christmas reminds us that God entrusted His Son to human hands knowing those hands were fragile. The Incarnation did not wait for perfect disciples; it created them through mercy, repentance, and perseverance.

The eleven pipers continue to play.

Their song did not stop because one voice fell silent. Fidelity means continuing the mission even when betrayal wounds the heart. The

Apostles would soon scatter in fear, yet they would return — forgiven, strengthened, and sent forth.

The Church survives not because her members are flawless, but because Christ is faithful.

Modern man often confuses disappointment with disbelief. He leaves not because Christ has failed, but because men have. Christmas calls us back to the essential truth: our faith rests not on personalities, but on a Person.

The eleven teach us that holiness is not immunity from failure, but perseverance after it.

When one falls, others must stand. When trust is broken, faith must deepen. When scandal darkens the path, fidelity must light the way forward.

Prayer

Lord Jesus,
faithful even when Your own were unfaithful,
strengthen my loyalty to You.
Keep me from judging Your truth
by the weakness of Your followers.
Give me the courage to remain,
to forgive, and to serve,
even when faith is tested.
Amen.

The Church did not survive because no one failed,
but because some remained faithful.

DAY 12

The Twelve Drummers Drumming — The Faith Proclaimed to the World

Truth, once received, must be proclaimed.

The carol reaches its crescendo with *twelve drummers drumming* — not a gentle image, but a commanding one. Drums announce. They gather. They summon. Beneath their rhythm lies the fullness of Christian proclamation: the **Twelve Apostles** and, by extension, the **Articles of Faith** entrusted to the Church.

Christianity was never meant to remain private.

Christ did not leave behind a philosophy, but a foundation. He built His Church upon twelve men — weak, fearful, and imperfect — and entrusted them with the truth that would change the world. What they received in silence, they proclaimed aloud. What they believed in secret, they preached in public. What they learned at Christmas, they announced at Pentecost.

The Apostles did not invent the faith; they *delivered* it.

This is why the Church has always insisted on doctrine. Love without truth becomes sentiment. Zeal without belief becomes noise. The Articles of Faith are not burdens imposed upon the mind; they are the rhythm that keeps the Gospel from dissolving into confusion.

The drummers do not improvise. They keep time.

So too the Apostles safeguarded the faith — not as museum curators, but as witnesses willing to suffer for what they proclaimed.

Nearly all would seal their testimony with blood. The Child once adored in Bethlehem would one day be preached to the nations as Lord and Savior.

Christmas, therefore, ends not in silence, but in proclamation.

The Incarnation demands response. The faith received must be professed. The truth believed must be lived and spoken. To celebrate Christmas fully is to join the Apostles in their mission — to let the rhythm of the Gospel shape every word, choice, and sacrifice.

The Twelve Days end where the Church begins: sent forth.

Prayer

Lord Jesus,
who entrusted Your truth to the Apostles,
strengthen my faith in all that You have revealed.
Give me courage to profess the truth without compromise,
humility to live it with charity,
and fidelity to pass it on intact.
May my life echo the Gospel
like a steady drumbeat in the world.
Amen.

Truth is not meant to be hidden in the heart alone,
but proclaimed to the world with courage and conviction.

CONCLUSION

Every Day is Christmas

Christmas does not end when the decorations come down.

The world treats Christmas as an interruption — a pause in ordinary time, a brief return to warmth before life resumes as usual. The Church knows better. Christmas is not an interruption of reality; it is the *revelation* of reality.

God did not enter time so that we might visit Him once a year. He entered time so that we might live with Him always.

The mystery celebrated at Christmas is not confined to Bethlehem. It continues wherever Christ is welcomed, received, and carried into the world. The Child laid in the manger still seeks room — not in inns, but in hearts. The question Christmas leaves us with is not whether Christ was born, but whether He is allowed to live again in us.

This is why the Church stretches Christmas across days, octaves, and feasts. Sacred time teaches sacred truth. The mystery must be lived before it can be understood. What begins in wonder must mature into witness.

Every day becomes Christmas when Christ is born anew through the sacraments.

In the Eucharist, the Word once again becomes Flesh — not symbolically, but truly. As Mary once gave her body so that Christ might enter the world, the Church now offers Him so that the world might be transformed. Each Mass is Bethlehem renewed. Each Communion is a quiet Nativity.

But Christmas does not remain on the altar.

Christ is given so that He may be carried. What was received in adoration must be lived in action. Love that remains private withers; love that is shared multiplies. The Incarnation demands imitation. As God once entered our humanity, so now He asks to enter the world through us.

Mary teaches us this final lesson. She did not keep the Word for herself. She bore Him into daily life — into travel, work, sorrow, and joy. Her "yes" did not end at Christmas; it became a way of living.

So too with us.

When faith endures after the season fades, Christmas remains. When charity persists beyond sentiment, Christmas continues. When Christ is carried into suffering, misunderstanding, and service, Christmas is fulfilled.

The Twelve Days may end, but the mission does not.

Every day is Christmas when Christ is allowed to live again — in word, in sacrament, and in love — through those who have received Him.

CHAPTER 13

Family Devotions at the Crib

1. Blessing of the Nativity Scene

(Adapted from traditional Catholic prayers, with Sheen's spirit of reflection)

Leader: Our help is in the name of the Lord.

All: Who made heaven and earth.

Leader: Almighty God, bless this crib and all who look upon it. As we gaze on this humble manger, may we remember the poverty of Bethlehem and the love that stooped so low to dwell among us.

All: May Christ be born anew in our hearts.

Leader: May this crib remind us that the glory of God is found in simplicity, humility, and love. May it inspire us to welcome Him with joy and to share His peace with others.

All: Come, Lord Jesus. Dwell in our homes, and reign in our hearts. Amen.

2. Christmas Eve Family Prayer at the Crib

1. Gather the family around the Nativity scene before Midnight Mass or Christmas dinner.

2. Read **Luke 2:1–20** aloud.

3. Place the figure of the Christ Child in the manger.

4. Together, pray:

All: Lord Jesus, we welcome You with joy. As the shepherds adored You in humility and the Magi honored You with gifts, so we come to offer You our hearts. Be Emmanuel in our family, bringing peace, unity, and love. Amen.

Sing a carol together (e.g., *Silent Night* or *O Come All Ye Faithful*).

3. Daily Family Prayer at the Crib

All together:

- One Our Father

- One Hail Mary

- One Glory Be

Leader: Eternal Word made flesh,

All: Dwell in our home today.

Leader: Holy Family of Nazareth,

All: Pray for us and guide our family.

(Optional: Each family member may place a small "gift" — written intention, act of charity, or prayer card — in a basket near the crib.)

4. Prayer of Consecration to the Holy Family

Jesus, Mary, and Joseph, we consecrate our family to your care. Protect us in our trials, guide us in our decisions, and unite us in your love.

May our home be a Nazareth, where Christ is honored, Mary is loved, and Joseph is trusted as guardian and guide.

Amen.

5. Reflection with Fulton Sheen

"The modern family is crumbling because it has forgotten Nazareth. God Himself chose to enter a family... The recovery of family life begins with a crib in which Christ is honored, a Mother who loves, and a father who provides and protects."

— *The World's First Love*

CHAPTER 14

Hymns and Carols
for Prayer

1. O Come, O Come, Emmanuel (Advent Hymn)

O come, O come, Emmanuel,
and ransom captive Israel,
that mourns in lonely exile here,
until the Son of God appear.

Refrain:

Rejoice! Rejoice! Emmanuel
shall come to thee, O Israel.

2. Come, Thou Long-Expected Jesus

Come, Thou long-expected Jesus,
born to set Thy people free;
from our fears and sins release us,
let us find our rest in Thee.

3. *Silent Night* (Christmas Hymn)

Silent night, holy night,
all is calm, all is bright.
Round yon Virgin, Mother and Child,
Holy Infant so tender and mild,
sleep in heavenly peace,
sleep in heavenly peace.

4. O Come, All Ye Faithful (Adeste Fideles)

O come, all ye faithful, joyful and triumphant,
O come ye, O come ye to Bethlehem;
Come and behold Him, born the King of Angels;
O come, let us adore Him,
O come, let us adore Him,
O come, let us adore Him, Christ the Lord.

5. Hark! The Herald Angels Sing

Hark! the herald angels sing,
"Glory to the new-born King;
peace on earth, and mercy mild,
God and sinners reconciled!"
Joyful, all ye nations, rise,
join the triumph of the skies;
with angelic hosts proclaim,
"Christ is born in Bethlehem!"

6. What Child Is This?

What Child is this, who, laid to rest,
on Mary's lap is sleeping?
Whom angels greet with anthems sweet,
while shepherds watch are keeping?

Refrain:

This, this is Christ the King,
whom shepherds guard and angels sing;
haste, haste, to bring Him laud,
the Babe, the Son of Mary.

CHAPTER 15

Prayers for Advent and Christmas

❧

1. The "O Antiphons" (Dec. 17–23)

Prayed at Vespers in the last week of Advent, each antiphon invokes Christ under a messianic title. Fulton Sheen often stressed how every prophecy finds fulfillment in the Incarnation.

Dec. 17 – O Wisdom (Sapientia)

O Wisdom, coming forth from the mouth of the Most High, reaching from one end to the other mightily, and sweetly ordering all things: come and teach us the way of prudence.

Dec. 18 – O Lord (Adonai)

O Adonai, and leader of the house of Israel, who appeared to Moses in the fire of the burning bush and gave him the law on Sinai: come to redeem us with outstretched arm.

Dec. 19 – O Root of Jesse (Radix Jesse)

O Root of Jesse, standing as a sign among the peoples; before you kings will shut their mouths, to you the nations will make their prayer: come and deliver us, and delay no longer.

Dec. 20 – O Key of David (Clavis David)

O Key of David and sceptre of the house of Israel; you open and no one can shut; you shut and no one can open: come and free the prisoner from the prison house.

Dec. 21 – O Dayspring (Oriens)

O Morning Star, splendor of light eternal and sun of righteousness: come and enlighten those who dwell in darkness and the shadow of death.

Dec. 22 – O King of the Nations (Rex Gentium)

O King of the nations, and their desire, the cornerstone making both one: come and save the human race, which you fashioned from clay.

Dec. 23 – O Emmanuel

O Emmanuel, our King and Lawgiver, the hope of the nations and their Saviour: come and save us, O Lord our God.

2. Advent Prayer for Watchfulness

Lord Jesus, teach me to wait with joy, to watch with love, and to welcome You in the silence of my heart.

Let every day of this Advent be a manger where You may find room to dwell. Amen.

(Inspired by Sheen: "The Advent spirit is vigilance... we wait not in fear, but in joy.")

3. Christmas Novena Prayer

(To be prayed nine days before Christmas)

O Divine Infant Jesus, at Bethlehem You came to dwell among us, humble and poor, yet rich in love.

Prepare my heart to be Your dwelling place.

Grant me the grace to imitate Mary's fiat, Joseph's trust, and the shepherds' humility.

May Your birth bring peace to my soul, and may my life proclaim that You are Emmanuel, God with us.

Amen.

4. Prayer Before the Crib

Eternal Word made flesh, as I kneel before Your manger, I see the shadow of the Cross.

You came not to be served, but to serve, not only to live among us, but to die for us.

Accept my love, my prayers, and my life, as I adore You in Your poverty and welcome You into my heart.

Amen.

5. Short Ejaculations (for daily use)

1. *Come, Lord Jesus.*

2. *Emmanuel, God with us, dwell in my heart.*

3. *O Infant King, reign in me today.*

4. *From the manger to the Cross, be my Savior and my friend.*

CHAPTER 16

Fulton Sheen on the Incarnation

1. The Humility of Bethlehem

"The infinite God became an infant. Eternity entered time, and the Word was made flesh. The majesty of heaven was wrapped in swaddling clothes and laid in a manger."

— *Life of Christ*

Reflection: At Christmas, God chose humility, so we could approach Him without fear.

2. The Two Births of Christ

"There are two births of Christ: one unto the world in Bethlehem; the other in the soul, when it is spiritually reborn. What good would it be if Christ were born in Bethlehem a thousand times, if He is not born in us?"

—*Christmas Inspirations*

Reflection: Bethlehem must happen again in your heart today.

3. The Manger and the Cross

"The manger and the Cross are of the same wood. The crib and the Cross are but two points along the same line."

— Life of Christ

Reflection: The joy of Christmas is inseparable from the sacrifice of Calvary.

4. Mary's Fiat

"Mary said Fiat because she was full of grace. Her whole life was a preparation for that yes, and through her yes, God entered the world."

— The World's First Love

Reflection: Every Christian is called to echo Mary's surrender.

5. Joseph's Obedience

"Joseph suffered a crucifixion of the mind. How could he reconcile Mary's sanctity with what appeared to be evidence to the contrary? But once God spoke, Joseph obeyed without hesitation."

— Life of Christ

Reflection: Silence and trust make the heart ready for God's plan.

6. The Poverty of Christ's Birth

"Divinity is always where you least expect to find it. The stable was not a sign of poverty, but of glory. The world rejected Him, but God's plan of love was not changed."

— Life of Christ

Reflection: The world may overlook Him, but Christ still chooses to dwell with us.

7. The Shadow of Suffering

"The Magi brought myrrh for His burial. Even in their joy, they proclaimed His sacrifice. From the beginning, Bethlehem was under the shadow of the Cross."

— *Christmas Inspirations*

Reflection: The Child who brings joy also bears the weight of our sins.

8. The Eternal Present

"Christmas is not just a memory; it is a reality. Christ lives on, and wherever He is received, it is Christmas again."

— *Christmas Inspirations*

Reflection: Every Eucharist is Bethlehem made present.

9. Emmanuel, God With Us

"Christmas is the meeting of opposites: eternity and time, divinity and humanity, majesty and humility. That is why it changes history itself into B.C. and A.D."

— *Life of Christ*

Reflection: Christ's coming is not just history — it is your story.

CHAPTER 17

Scripture for Reflection

1. The Promise of the Messiah

Isaiah 9:2, 6–7

"The people who walked in darkness have seen a great light; those who dwelt in a land of deep darkness, on them has light shined.

For to us a child is born, to us a son is given; and the government will be upon his shoulder, and his name will be called "Wonderful Counselor, Mighty God, Everlasting Father, Prince of Peace."

Of the increase of his government and of peace there will be no end, upon the throne of David, and over his kingdom, to establish it, and to uphold it with justice and with righteousness from this time forth and for evermore. The zeal of the Lord of hosts will do this."

Sheen's Insight:

"The Old Testament is incomplete without the New. It is like a riddle awaiting its answer. Advent is the season of expectancy when the answer is revealed in Christ."

Reflection Question: Where in my life do I most need Christ's light to break through the darkness?

2. Mary's Fiat

Luke 1:26–38
The Birth of Jesus Foretold

"In the sixth month, the angel Gabriel was sent from God to a city of Galilee named Nazareth, to a virgin betrothed to a man whose name was Joseph, of the house of David; and the virgin's name was Mary. And he came to her and said, "Hail, full of grace, the Lord is with you!"

But she was greatly troubled at the saying, and considered in her mind what sort of greeting this might be. And the angel said to her, "Do not be afraid, Mary, for you have found favor with God. And behold, you will conceive in your womb and bear a son, and you shall call his name Jesus. He will be great, and will be called the Son of the Most High; and the Lord God will give to him the throne of his father David, and he will reign over the house of Jacob for ever; and of his kingdom there will be no end."

And Mary said to the angel, "How can this be, since I have no husband? "And the angel said to her, "The Holy Spirit will come upon you, and the power of the Most High will overshadow you; therefore the child to be born[d] will be called holy, the Son of God.

*And behold, your kinswoman Elizabeth in her old age has also conceived a son; and this is the sixth month with her who was called barren. For with God nothing will be impossible." And Mary said, **"Behold, I am the handmaid of the Lord; let it be to me according to your word."** And the angel departed from her."*

Sheen's Insight:

"Mary's Fiat was the fruit of her fullness of grace. Her whole life was a preparation for that moment of surrender."

Reflection Question: What part of my life is God asking me to surrender to Him with trust?

3. Joseph's Obedience

"Now the birth of Jesus Christ took place in this way. When his mother Mary had been betrothed to Joseph, before they came together, she was found to be with child of the Holy Spirit; and her husband Joseph, being a just man and unwilling to put her to shame, resolved to send her away quietly. But as he considered this, behold, an angel of the Lord appeared to him in a dream, saying, "Joseph, son of David, do not fear to take Mary your wife, for that which is conceived in her is of the Holy Spirit; she will bear a son, and you shall call his name Jesus, for he will save his people from their sins." All this took place to fulfil what the Lord had spoken by the prophet:

"Behold, a virgin shall conceive and bear a son, and his name shall be called Emmanuel" (which means, God with us). **When Joseph woke from sleep, he did as the angel of the Lord commanded him;** *he took his wife, but knew her not until she had borne a son; and he called his name Jesus."*

Sheen's Insight:

"Joseph obeyed in silence, without hesitation. His greatness was not in words, but in fidelity."

Reflection Question: Do I obey God promptly, or do I delay until I feel more secure?

4. The Birth of Jesus

Luke 2:6–7

"And while they were there, the time came for her to be delivered. And she gave birth to her firstborn son and wrapped him in swaddling cloths, and laid him in a manger, because there was no place for them in the inn."

Sheen's Insight:

"The saddest line of history: there was no room in the inn. The tragedy was not hostility, but preoccupation."

Reflection Question: What distractions keep me from making room for Christ?

5. The Shepherds

Luke 2:15–16

"When the angels went away from them into heaven, the shepherds said to one another, "Let us go over to Bethlehem and see this thing that has happened, which the Lord has made known to us." And they went with haste, and found Mary and Joseph, and the babe lying in a manger."

Sheen's Insight:

"The shepherds heard because they were simple. God is found by the humble of heart."

Reflection Question: How can I cultivate simplicity and humility to encounter Christ?

6. The Magi

Matthew 2:10–11

"When they saw the star, they rejoiced exceedingly with great joy; and going into the house they saw the child with Mary his mother, and they fell down and worshiped him. Then, opening their treasures, they offered him gifts, gold and frankincense and myrrh."

Sheen's Insight:

"The Magi brought gold for His kingship, incense for His priesthood, and myrrh for His burial. Even at the cradle, the Cross was present."

Reflection Question: What gift of my life can I lay before the Child this Christmas?

7. The Word Made Flesh

John 1:14

"And the Word became flesh and dwelt among us, full of grace and truth; we have beheld his glory, glory as of the only Son from the Father."

Sheen's Insight:

"Christmas is not a sentimental memory; it is the shocking humility of God taking on our flesh to dwell among us."

Reflection Question: Do I see Christ's presence in the ordinary moments of daily life?

8. Simeon's Prophecy

Luke 2:34–35

And Simeon blessed them and said to Mary his mother, "Behold, this child is set for the fall and rising of many in Israel, and for a sign that is spoken against (and a sword will pierce through your own soul also), that thoughts out of many hearts may be revealed."

Sheen's Insight:

"The shadow of the Cross fell across Bethlehem. From the first, He was destined for sacrifice."

Reflection Question: How can I unite my sufferings with the Child who came to embrace the Cross?

Scripture Index

Old Testament

- Isaiah 7:14 — A virgin shall conceive

- Isaiah 9:2, 6–7 — The people who walked in darkness

- Isaiah 11:1 — A shoot from the stump of Jesse

- Isaiah 40:3–5 — A voice cries in the wilderness

Gospels

- Matthew 1:18–24 — Joseph's obedience

- Matthew 2:10–11 — The Magi's gifts

- Luke 1:26–38 — Mary's Fiat

- Luke 2:6–7 — No room at the inn

- Luke 2:15–16 — The shepherds at the crib

- Luke 2:34–35 — Simeon's prophecy

- Luke 2:51–52 — The child grew in wisdom

- John 1:1, 14 — The Word was made flesh

Epistles

- Romans 8:22–25 — Creation groans in hope

- Galatians 4:4–6 — Born of a woman, born under the law

- Philippians 2:6-8 — He humbled Himself

CHAPTER 18

A Short Guide to Making an Advent & Christmas Holy Hour

Inspired by Archbishop Fulton J. Sheen, who made a daily Holy Hour before the Blessed Sacrament.

1. Begin in Silence

- Enter the church or prayer space quietly.

- If before the Blessed Sacrament, kneel in adoration.

- If at home, place a crucifix or Nativity scene before you and light a candle.

- Pray slowly: *"Come, Lord Jesus."*

2. Scripture Reading (10 minutes)

Choose a passage fitting the season:

- **Advent**: Isaiah 9:2–7; Luke 1:26–38

- **Christmas**: Luke 2:1–20; John 1:1–14

- **Beyond Christmas**: Galatians 4:4–6; Luke 2:34–35

Read slowly. Pause. Let one phrase echo in your heart.

3. Meditation with Fulton Sheen (10 minutes)

- Reflect on one of Sheen's insights:

  "The manger and the Cross are of the same wood."
  "What good would it be if Christ were born in Bethlehem a thousand times, if He is not born in us?"

- Ask: What is God saying to me through this?

4. Personal Conversation (20 minutes)

- Speak to Christ as you would to a friend.

- Share your joys, your struggles, your hopes.

- Listen in silence for His response.

5. Acts of Love and Reparation (10 minutes)

- Offer prayers of adoration: *"Jesus, I love You."*

- Make reparation for sins (your own and the world's).

- Unite yourself with the Holy Family at Bethlehem and Nazareth.

6. Conclude with a Prayer of Consecration

Lord Jesus,
born in Bethlehem and present in the Eucharist,
I adore You and I welcome You into my heart.
Mary and Joseph, teach me to keep watch with love.
May every Holy Hour prepare me for eternity,
where I shall behold Your face forever.

Amen.

7. Optional Hymn

Close with a carol or hymn: *Silent Night, O Come All Ye Faithful, or Adeste Fideles.*

PART V
Treasury of Christmas Meditations
For Prayer and Reflection

DAILY REFLECTIONS

Pause and Rest
in the Promise

Throughout this book, you will find short daily reflections
placed at the end of each major section
(Advent, Christmas, and the days that follow).

These reflections are meant to be prayed slowly.

You may use them:

- One or two per day

- During a Holy Hour

- In evening prayer before rest

- Shared with family or parish groups

- As quiet preparation before Mass

There is no need to rush.
Rest with the reflection, sit with it, let it speak to the heart.

As Archbishop Fulton J. Sheen wrote:

*"We must let God be the sculptor of the soul.
Our task is to be still enough to be shaped."*

Read slowly. Pause. Receive.

Let these meditations deepen your longing for Christ
and your desire to welcome Him when He comes.

"Come, Lord Jesus."

The Waiting of the World

————————

Before Christ came, humanity waited — sometimes knowingly, sometimes unknowingly — for Someone who could restore what was broken.

We still feel that longing today.
We long for peace.
We long for healing.
We long for meaning.

And into that longing, God comes.
Not to remove our hunger, but to **fill it with Himself**.

Waiting is not a failure of faith.
Waiting is the posture of the heart that trusts God's timing.

The manger teaches us that **God arrives at the right moment** — not early, not late, but when love is ready to be received.

May we find His presence today, even in the places we least expect.

Lord Jesus, grant me the grace to love You more today than yesterday, and more tomorrow than today.

Amen.

The Silence of Bethlehem

———————

The night Christ was born was not loud with triumph — it was quiet.
No trumpets, no crowds, no announcements across the earth.
Only the soft breathing of animals, the whisper of straw, the stillness
of night.

God came in silence so that **we would learn where to listen**.

The deepest things in life are spoken quietly —
love, sorrow, beauty, repentance, longing.

If we want to find God, we must make room for silence.

Not the silence of emptiness, but the silence of **attention** —
the silence that listens for God's footsteps.

Bethlehem teaches us that God does not shout.
He waits for the heart that is still enough to hear Him.

May we find His presence today, even in the places we least expect.

*Lord Jesus, grant me the grace to love You more today than
yesterday, and more tomorrow than today.*

Amen.

The Inn and the Manger

———————————

There was no room in the inn — but there was room in the manger.

The inn was crowded, busy, filled with noise, movement, and distraction.

The manger was quiet, poor, forgotten — but open.

The heart can be like either place.

Sometimes we fill our lives so completely — with plans, anxieties, possessions, and noise — that there is no room for God.

Yet He never forces His way in.

He looks for the open space, however humble.

The place where Christ is born is not the place of perfection, but the place of **welcome**.

If we offer Him even a small space of silence, of kindness, of prayer, of surrender,

He will fill it with Himself.

May we find His presence today, even in the places we least expect.

Lord Jesus, grant me the grace to love You more today than yesterday, and more tomorrow than today.

Amen.

The Paradise God Prepared

Before God created Adam, He prepared a garden — a paradise of beauty.

Before God came to us in the flesh, He prepared **Mary** — a paradise of grace.

She is the living sanctuary,
the garden where the new Adam would walk,
the dwelling where God would take on our humanity.

Mary is not distant or unreachable.
She is the place where love learned to beat with a human heart.

To welcome Mary is to draw near to Christ,
just as He drew near to us through her.

She does not replace Him.
She reveals Him.

May we find His presence today, even in the places we least expect.

Lord Jesus, grant me the grace to love You more today than yesterday, and more tomorrow than today.

Amen.

The Poverty of the Manger

Christ was born in poverty — not because God romanticizes hardship, but because **He wanted nothing to stand between Him and the human heart.**

If He had come in splendor, the proud would have claimed Him.

If He had come in power, the strong would have gathered around Him.

But He came in humility, so that **all might draw near.**

The manger teaches us that God does not wait for perfect conditions before He enters our lives.

He comes into whatever is real — whatever is ordinary — whatever is small.

He sanctifies what the world overlooks.

The place where Christ is welcomed becomes holy.

May we find His presence today, even in the places we least expect.

Lord Jesus, grant me the grace to love You more today than yesterday, and more tomorrow than today.

Amen.

The Shepherd's Awakening

The shepherds were not scholars or rulers or elites.

They were ordinary people keeping watch in the quiet of night.

But it was **to them** that Heaven opened.

Why?
Because their hearts were awake.
Because they were attentive.
Because silence had prepared them to hear God.

God often comes to us in moments that seem small — a whisper of conscience, a moment of beauty, an unexpected stirring of hope.

To notice Him, we do not need brilliance.
We need **openness**.

The shepherds teach us how to receive Christmas:
not with analysis, but with wonder.

May we find His presence today, even in the places we least expect.

Lord Jesus, grant me the grace to love You more today than yesterday, and more tomorrow than today.

Amen.

The Wonder of the Child

———————

The infinite God became a child.

Not because He needed to, but because **we needed Him to**.

A child disarms us.
A child does not intimidate or overwhelm.
A child invites tenderness, affection, gentleness, love.

God knows the human heart.
He knows that love grows easiest where there is humility and trust.

So He came small.

So that we would not be afraid.
So that we would learn that **God is love**, and love is never proud.

The manger is not just a scene — it is a message:
Come close. Do not fear. I am yours.

May we find His presence today, even in the places we least expect.

Lord Jesus, grant me the grace to love You more today than yesterday, and more tomorrow than today.

Amen.

The Joy That Cannot Be Taken

The joy of Christmas is not temporary, like celebration or excitement.
It is deeper — quiet, steady, rooted in **God-with-us**.

This joy does not depend on circumstances.
It does not fade when life becomes difficult.
It does not disappear when feelings shift.

It remains, because it comes from the One who remains.

Joy is not what we feel — joy is *Who* we have.

And we have Christ.

If He is with us, then even in sorrow there can be peace,
and even in hardship there can be hope.

This is the joy the world cannot take.

May we find His presence today, even in the places we least expect.

Lord Jesus, grant me the grace to love You more today than yesterday, and more tomorrow than today.

Amen.

Christmas Is for the Broken

———————————

Christ did not come for those who believe themselves good enough. He came for those who know they need mercy.

Christmas is not the feast of the perfect — it is the feast of the hopeful.

The manger is not surrounded by the proud,
but by shepherds, wanderers, and seekers.

God is drawn to the humble heart,
the heart that says:
Lord, I need You.

The joy of Christmas begins where self-reliance ends.

May we find His presence today, even in the places we least expect.

Lord Jesus, grant me the grace to love You more today than yesterday, and more tomorrow than today.

Amen.

The Humility That Sees the Child

The proud man cannot recognize God in the manger.
He looks for kings in palaces, not in straw.
He expects wisdom to arrive with applause, not with silence.

But God hides Himself in littleness
so that only the humble will find Him.

To enter Bethlehem, one must **stoop**.
To recognize Christ, one must **kneel**.

The one who bows discovers that the cave is not darkness —
but the doorway into light.

Christmas teaches us that God does not ask us to be great —
only to be small enough to receive Him.

May we find His presence today, even in the places we least expect.

Lord Jesus, grant me the grace to love You more today than yesterday, and more tomorrow than today.

Amen.

Where Love and Child Are One

In most births, love rises from earth to heaven.
Human love reaches upward and asks for blessing.

But at Christmas, **love came down**.

The Child of Bethlehem was not simply the result of human longing
— He was the answer to it.

Mary did not stumble into motherhood.
She **willed** it in love:
"Let it be done unto me according to Your word."

Her motherhood began not in her body, but in her **heart**.

And the Child she bore was not merely hers — He was **God's love made visible**.

Where love is pure and surrendered,
God makes Himself known.
In the manger,
Love and Child are one.

May we find His presence today, even in the places we least expect.

Lord Jesus, grant me the grace to love You more today than yesterday, and more tomorrow than today.

Amen.

The Mother Resembles the Child

When a child is born, we ask,
"Whom does the baby resemble?"

But at Christmas, it is different.

Christ did not come to imitate Mary.
Mary was formed to reflect **Him**.

Her purity, her tenderness, her humility — these were not merely her
own virtues, but the radiance of the One she carried.

She held Him in her arms,
but she was the one being shaped.

Most mothers look up to heaven.
Mary looked **down** — for Heaven was in her arms.

To love Mary is simply to learn how to love Jesus
as she loved Him.

May we find His presence today, even in the places we least expect.

*Lord Jesus, grant me the grace to love You more today than
yesterday, and more tomorrow than today.*

Amen.

Why We Give Gifts at Christmas

We give gifts because **God first gave Himself**.

Love always desires to give.

And the greatest gift is presence — to say with our actions: "You matter. You are loved."

Every small gift at Christmas is a reflection of the Gift in the manger — God become man, so that humanity may become like God.

May we find His presence today, even in the places we least expect.

Lord Jesus, grant me the grace to love You more today than yesterday, and more tomorrow than today.

Amen.

The New Melody of Christmas

Before there was music on earth, there was music in God — a harmony that filled creation with beauty and order. Every creature was meant to play its part in this symphony of love.

But when the human heart turned away, the music broke. A discord entered the world — a note of pride, of self, of separation. And once the harmony was wounded, humanity could not restore it by itself.

So God began a new song.

Not with power.
Not with command.
But with a Child.

The first note of the new melody was a cry in Bethlehem — soft, small, and pure. In that Child, God wrote a new beginning. A new humanity. A new way of loving.

Those who join their lives to His become part of that music — no longer "once-born," but "twice-born," no longer alone, but taken up into the great harmony of Christ.

Christmas is the invitation to let our discord become part of His song —

to let grace rewrite what sin has damaged, to let mercy soften what pride has hardened, to let Christ tune our hearts again.

Every yes to Him becomes a note in the new melody of love.

May we find His presence today, even in the places we least expect.

The Ones Who Kneel

The first to find the Christ Child were not the powerful, the influential, or the self-assured. They were two groups who, though very different, shared something essential: **humility**.

The Shepherds came with empty hands.
The Wise Men came with full hands.
But both came with **open hearts**.

The Shepherds were the ones who *knew they knew nothing*.
Their lives were simple, their wisdom unpolished, their vision sharpened not by books but by quiet nights under the stars. They recognized the voice of God because they had learned to listen.

The Wise Men were the ones who *knew they did not know everything*.
They had searched the skies, studied the patterns of the universe, and discovered the limits of their own brilliance. Their learning led them not to pride, but to wonder.

Both knelt.

Christmas is never found by the proud.
Not by the self-satisfied.
Not by the one who believes he has no need of God.

Christmas is found by the searching heart— the one hungry for meaning, longing for truth, ready to kneel.

The Shepherds did not understand everything, but they came.
The Wise Men did not see the whole road, but they followed the star.

Those who kneel will always find the Child.

May we find His presence today, even in the places we least

The Gift That Teaches Us to Give

We give gifts at Christmas
because we have first **received a Gift**.

God gave Himself to us — not in power,
but in tenderness;
not in majesty,
but in vulnerability.

This Gift came wrapped in swaddling clothes
and laid in a manger.

Love always gives.
And so we give.

Not to match the greatness of His Gift — for that is impossible —
but to let love overflow from the heart.

Every true gift is an echo of Bethlehem.

Let your giving be love — not price, not performance, not obligation
— but love.

The King We Were Made to Find

Even those who claim to reject kings
cannot escape the longing to admire, to exalt, to adore.

We crown celebrities, praise leaders, honor champions — because
the heart knows it was made to bow before greatness.

But the true King does not appear in splendor or force.
He comes in humility, in gentleness, in silence.

His throne is a manger.
His crown is love.

To find Him, we must go where the proud do not go — to the quiet
places where the humble adore.

There, the heart knows its King.

Discovering God at Christmas
by Archbishop Fulton J. Sheen

There were only two classes of people who heard the cry Christmas night: shepherds and wise men.

Shepherds: those who know they know nothing.

Wise men: those who know they do not know everything.

Only the very simple and very learned discovered God

— never the man with one book.

The Journey of the Wise Men

The Wise Men travelled far — not guided by certainty, but by **trust**.
They followed a light in the sky because they sensed a greater light
waiting at its end.

They remind us that faith is a **journey**, not a possession.
We do not always see the destination clearly.
We take one step, then another.

The Wise Men did not find Christ in the palace where logic led them
— but in the humble place where **God** led them.

Our path to God may not look like we imagined.
But if we keep seeking, we will find Him — not always where we
expect, but always where we need.

May we find His presence today, even in the places we least expect.

*Lord Jesus, grant me the grace to love You more today than
yesterday, and more tomorrow than today.*

Amen.

The Light in the Darkness

The world into which Christ was born was not peaceful or pure.
It was weary, fractured, longing.

He did not wait for the world to become worthy — He came **into its darkness** to bring the light.

Light does not ask the darkness for permission.
It does not negotiate.
It simply shines — and the darkness cannot overcome it.

There are places within us that still long for that light:

- our fears
- our hidden wounds
- our unanswered questions
- our hopes waiting to wake again

Christ enters those places gently.

We do not have to remove the darkness first.
We only need to open the door.

May we find His presence today, even in the places we least expect.

Lord Jesus, grant me the grace to love You more today than yesterday, and more tomorrow than today.

Amen.

The Light That Enters the Cave

———————

Archbishop Fulton Sheen reminds us that the Light of Christ does not frighten the humble — only the proud.

The shepherds were not afraid to draw near.
They knew their need.
They went to the cave as beggars and returned as men reborn.

But others feared the Light.
Herod feared losing power.
The innkeeper feared discomfort.
The comfortable feared change.

The Light of Christ reveals — but it also heals.
It uncovers — but it also restores.

If we allow the Light to touch even the hidden places,
we will not shrink — we will shine.

May we find His presence today, even in the places we least expect.

Lord Jesus, grant me the grace to love You more today than yesterday, and more tomorrow than today.

Amen.

The Humble and the Wise

Those who came to the manger were not the proud, nor the self-sufficient.
It was the **shepherds** and the **wise men**:

- The shepherds came because they *knew they knew nothing.*

- The wise men came because they *knew they did not know everything.*

Both possessed **humility** — and humility opened the door to adoration.

Pride stands outside the stable and evaluates.
Humility kneels inside and worships.

Christmas is not found in learning, status, refinement, or intellect.
It is found in the soul that knows its need.

To kneel before the Christ Child is not to shrink — it is to stand in truth.

May we find His presence today, even in the places we least expect.

Lord Jesus, grant me the grace to love You more today than yesterday, and more tomorrow than today.

Amen.

The First Note in a New Symphony

God created the world in harmony — a perfect symphony of love
and order.

But humanity chose a different note — a discord born of pride.
And like a sound that echoes endlessly,
that disharmony spread through history.

Yet God did not abandon His work.
He began **a new composition**.

And the first note of this new song
was the cry of a Child in Bethlehem.

A melody of mercy.
A harmony of peace.
A music that invites all people
to return to love.

When we unite our lives to Him,
our broken notes are gathered
into His beautiful song.

May our hearts be tuned to His.

May we find His presence today, even in the places we least expect.

*Lord Jesus, grant me the grace to love You more today than
yesterday, and more tomorrow than today.*

Amen.

The Life That Spreads Like Light

Grace is not simply a teaching or a memory.
It is a **life** that flows from Christ to us.

Just as warmth spreads from fire,
or fragrance from a flower,
so the life of God spreads to those who draw near Him.

Christ became man so that God's own life
could pass into ours.

To be a Christian, then, is not only to admire Him — but to **receive Him**.

The more we stay close to Christ — in prayer, in silence, in charity —
the more His life becomes our own.

If we come near enough,
we will begin to love with His love.

A Love That Stoops

God's love does not remain distant.
It bends, it lowers, it stoops — all the way to a cradle of straw.

We often imagine that we must climb our way to God — through
effort, virtue, achievement, or strength.
But Christmas tells us: **God comes down to us**.

He comes not to overwhelm us, but to meet us where we are.
He chooses simplicity so that no one is intimidated.
He chooses littleness so that no one is afraid.

The God who stoops to us invites us to stoop to one another — to
serve, to forgive, to listen, to love.

May we find His presence today, even in the places we least expect.

*Lord Jesus, grant me the grace to love You more today than
yesterday, and more tomorrow than today.*

Amen.

The Gift of Adoration

When the Wise Men reached Bethlehem, they did not **ask** for anything.

They **offered** something: their worship.

True love does not begin with "What can I receive?"
It begins with "What can I give?"

Adoration is not flattery or obligation — it is the heart recognizing the One for whom it was made.

Kneeling is not humiliation — it is **freedom**,
because the soul bows only to the One worthy of worship.

The Wise Men teach us that the greatest gifts we bring to Christ are not gold or treasures — but **our hearts made humble in love.**

May we find His presence today, even in the places we least expect.

Lord Jesus, grant me the grace to love You more today than yesterday, and more tomorrow than today.

Amen.

The Cradle and the Cross

The wood of the manger
and the wood of the Cross
come from the same tree of love.

Christ accepted the stable at His birth
because hearts had no room for Him.

He accepted the Cross at His death
for the very same reason.

From the beginning,
He came to give Himself completely.

There is no tragedy in His life — only purpose,
only love freely offered.

For those who know themselves to be stables — places poor,
humble, and in need — His coming brings joy.

For where He is welcomed,
everything is made new.

Christmas: The Mother Resembles the Child

When a child is born, we look to see whom the child resembles.
But at Christmas, everything is reversed.

Christ did not come to resemble Mary.
Mary came to resemble Christ.

She was not the source of His holiness — He was the source of hers.

Sheen reminds us that Mary did not simply give Christ His physical life.
Christ first gave her the fullness of grace, so that she could be a fitting home for Him.
Her purity, her humility, her tenderness — these were reflections of the One she carried.

And here is the great paradox: Mothers often lift their children's eyes upward and say, "Heaven is above."

But when Mary held the Child in her arms,
she looked down to Heaven.

Christmas reveals a love that changes us from within.
The closer we draw to Christ, the more we resemble Him.

This is the true meaning of devotion to Mary — not to stop at her, but to learn from her how to hold Christ, how to love Him, how to resemble Him.

May we welcome Him in the quiet places of our hearts.

May we find His presence today, even in the places we least expect.

The House of Bread

Bethlehem means **"House of Bread."**
And the Child born there called Himself **the Bread of Life.**

He comes to feed the hunger that lies deeper than the body — the
hunger of the soul.

We can fill our days with activity, noise, experience, success,
and yet still feel a quiet emptiness within.

This hunger is holy.
It is the heart recognizing its need for God.

The manger is a table.
The Child is the Gift.

To receive Him is to be fed with life that does not fade.

May we find His presence today, even in the places we least expect.

*Lord Jesus, grant me the grace to love You more today than
yesterday, and more tomorrow than today.*

Amen.

The Silence of Mary

———————

Mary speaks little in the Gospels — not because she has nothing to say, but because love is often expressed best in **silence**.

In silence, she received the angel's message.
In silence, she carried God within her.
In silence, she stood by the Cross.

Silence is not emptiness — it is space where God can speak.

If we fill our lives with noise — constant movement, constant demands, constant distraction — we may miss the whisper of God.

Mary teaches us a different way:

- to listen,

- to wait,

- to trust,

- to ponder.

Her silence is not withdrawal;
it is **communion**.

May we find His presence today, even in the places we least expect.

Lord Jesus, grant me the grace to love You more today than yesterday, and more tomorrow than today.

Amen.

The Hidden Years

Most of Christ's life was hidden — quiet, ordinary, unseen.

No crowds.
No miracles.
No public teaching.

Just love — lived faithfully, day by day.

This tells us something profound:
Holiness is not found only in extraordinary moments.
It is found in **the ordinary**, offered to God.

The home, the workplace, the conversations we repeat,
the duties we carry — these are places where love can grow.

Bethlehem leads to Nazareth.
The wonder of Christmas leads to the simplicity of daily life.

God is not far from our routine.
He is *in* it.

May we find His presence today, even in the places we least expect.

Lord Jesus, grant me the grace to love You more today than yesterday, and more tomorrow than today.

Amen.

The Joy That Comes from Surrender

Mary did not choose the easy path.
She chose the **true** one.

Her "Yes" carried weight:
misunderstanding,
uncertainty,
poverty,
sacrifice.

Yet her soul **rejoiced**.

Joy does not come from comfort or convenience.
Joy comes from **saying yes to God,**
even when we do not see the full picture.

We may not know where the path leads —
but if we walk it with Him,
it will always lead to joy.

May we find His presence today, even in the places we least expect.

Lord Jesus, grant me the grace to love You more today than yesterday, and more tomorrow than today.

Amen.

The Poverty of God

Christ chose poverty — not because poverty is comfortable,
but because **love desires nothing to separate it from the beloved**.

By becoming poor, Christ removed every barrier between Himself
and us.

He became accessible, touchable, approachable.

No throne separates us from Him.
No magnificence overwhelms us.
No greatness frightens us.

He comes to us needing — so that we will not fear needing Him.

The poverty of Bethlehem is the language of love:
I come close so you may come close.

May we find His presence today, even in the places we least expect.

***Lord Jesus, grant me the grace to love You more today than
yesterday, and more tomorrow than today.***

Amen.

Mary, the First Monstrance

Before Christ was lifted in the monstrance upon the altar,
He was lifted in the arms of His Mother.

Mary was the first to **carry Him**,
the first to **adore Him**,
the first to **offer Him** to the world.

Her whole life was a silent Eucharist:

- She received Him.

- She loved Him.

- She gave Him.

When we gaze upon Christ in the Eucharist,
we are invited to love Him as she did — with a heart that is quiet,
trusting, and full.

To love Mary does not take us away from Jesus — it places us beside
Him.

May we find His presence today, even in the places we least expect.

*Lord Jesus, grant me the grace to love You more today than
yesterday, and more tomorrow than today.*

Amen.

The Handmaid of the Lord

Mary called herself the **Handmaid of the Lord** — the one who
serves.

Her greatness is not in power,
position,
accomplishment,
or recognition.

Her greatness is in **availability**.

God does not need our strength.
He needs our **yes**.

Mary teaches us that holiness is not achieved — it is **received**,
by allowing God to lead.

When we surrender our plans,
He gives us His peace.

May we find His presence today, even in the places we least expect.

*Lord Jesus, grant me the grace to love You more today than
yesterday, and more tomorrow than today.*

Amen.

Love Comes from Heaven

In most families, a child begins with the love of two hearts. There is tenderness, desire, and hope — and yet, even this love is fragile and limited.

Parents can long for a child, but life always arrives as mystery.

But the Birth of Christ was different.

Here, love did not rise from earth to heaven — **it came from heaven to earth**.

Mary did not simply discover life within her. She *willed* to receive the Life of God:

"Be it done unto me according to Thy word."

Her motherhood began not in the body, but in the heart.

The Holy Spirit overshadowed her, and in that holy surrender, **Love became Flesh.**

This is what Christmas reveals:

Love is not only something God gives. **Love is Who God is.**

And when Love takes flesh, Child and Love become one.

May that same Love be born in us — quietly, simply, wherever there is room.

When God Feels Far Away

There are seasons when God seems distant — not absent, but hidden.

We ache for Him.
We long for Him.
We remember a closeness we once knew.

This longing is not a failure of faith — it is faith in its most honest and tender form.

We do not grieve what we do not love.

The heart that laments God's hiddenness
is a heart in which God already dwells.

Sometimes the nearness of God is too deep for feelings.
Sometimes He comes to us disguised in silence.

If we continue to seek Him,
even longing becomes prayer.

May we find His presence today, even in the places we least expect.

Lord Jesus, grant me the grace to love You more today than yesterday, and more tomorrow than today.

Amen.

The Hidden God

For nine months, God was hidden in Mary.
For thirty years, God was hidden in Nazareth.
For centuries, God is hidden in the Eucharist.

God often works **quietly**,
patiently,
gently.

We want miracles, flashes, signs.
But God often moves in the slow growth of love.

Do not mistake **quiet** for **absence**.

The hidden God is the faithful God.
The God who dwells, stays, abides.

Holiness is not spectacular — it is steady.

May we find His presence today, even in the places we least expect.

Lord Jesus, grant me the grace to love You more today than yesterday, and more tomorrow than today.

Amen.

The Son of God, Our Brother

Christ did not only come to save us — He came to **stand with us**.

He knows our hunger,
our fear,
our laughter,
our sorrow.

He is not ashamed to call us His brothers and sisters.

Let us not treat Him as a distant figure,
but as One who walks beside us.

We belong to Him.
We are family.

May we find His presence today, even in the places we least expect.

Lord Jesus, grant me the grace to love You more today than yesterday, and more tomorrow than today.

Amen.

When the Heart Misses God

There are seasons when God feels distant — not gone, but hidden. The soul hungers and thirsts for something it can no longer touch, and the ache becomes its own form of prayer.

We do not mourn what we do not love.
We do not feel absence unless Presence once mattered.

There is a loneliness that comes from having known God, having tasted grace, having once been held close by the warmth of faith. The one who has loved deeply grieves more profoundly when love seems silent.

But this longing is not a failure of faith.
It *is* faith — waiting in the dark.

The soul that aches for God already belongs to Him. The pain is the proof. The yearning is the evidence. The emptiness is not the absence of God, but the space He is preparing to fill.

Christ does not avoid the places where we feel most alone.
He draws near there — quietly, gently, like a Child laid close to the heart.

When we cannot feel Him, He is often nearest.
When we cannot see Him, He may be standing just beyond the veil of our sorrow.
When we ache for Him, it is because His love has already claimed us.

The longing is not the end of faith.
It is the doorway to encounter.

May we find His presence today, even in the places we least expect.

When Fear Drives Us into Our Caves

Archbishop Fulton Sheen tells us that every age has its cave — the place where humanity hides from God.

In our time, the cave may not be made of stone,
but of distractions, noise, self-reliance, and guarded hearts.

We fear silence because silence reveals the soul.
We fear stillness because stillness invites God.

But Christ does not wait for us to emerge strong.
He enters the cave **with us**.

The Child of Bethlehem comes not to condemn our fear, but to banish it with love.

We do not have to be brave to welcome Him.
We only have to be willing.

May we find His presence today, even in the places we least expect.

Lord Jesus, grant me the grace to love You more today than yesterday, and more tomorrow than today.

Amen.

God Walked Our Earth

The universe is vast — full of stars, galaxies, and mysteries we cannot measure.

Yet God chose **our** small world.
He walked our roads, breathed our air,
felt fatigue, hunger, joy, loneliness, and hope.

Every religion tells the story of humanity seeking God.
Christmas tells the story of **God seeking humanity**.

Not from afar,
but up close.

The Creator placed His feet
upon the dust He Himself had formed.

The One who made the stars
walked beneath them.

He did not come to overwhelm us,
but to draw near enough
for us to love Him.

God walked our earth — and He walks it still
where hearts make room.

May we find His presence today, even in the places we least expect.

Lord Jesus, grant me the grace to love You more today than yesterday, and more tomorrow than today.

Amen.

His Name Shall Be Jesus

———————————

The Name **Jesus** is not simply a label — it is a mission.

It means: **God saves.**

Just as Joshua once led God's people
into the promised land,
Jesus leads us into the promise of eternal life.

Every time we speak His Name with love,
we call upon the One who:

seeks,
forgives,
heals,
and saves.

The simplest prayer in the world
is also the greatest:

Jesus.
May we find His presence today, even in the places we least expect.

Lord Jesus, grant me the grace to love You more today than
yesterday, and more tomorrow than today.

Amen.

The Brother Who Knows Our Hearts

Christ is **God with us** — but He is also **God like us**.

He knew hunger and weariness,
joy and sorrow,
laughter and tears.

There is no pain you can feel
that He has not carried in some way.
No loneliness He has not known.
No burden He has not shared.

He is not ashamed to call us His brothers and sisters.

The only question is whether we will treat Him
as family — or only as a distant acquaintance.

He waits for a place in our daily lives,
not just our Sunday prayers.

It's Free

We cannot lift ourselves to God.
So God came down to us.

Grace is not earned.
It is received.
It is **gift**.

But love never forces.
It invites.

When we surrender — even a little — God lifts us more than we
could lift ourselves in a lifetime.

To give Him your heart
is to discover what freedom truly is.

May we find His presence today, even in the places we least expect.

*Lord Jesus, grant me the grace to love You more today than
yesterday, and more tomorrow than today.*

Amen.

Where Is He Who Is Born King?

———————

Every soul longs for a king — someone worthy of love, loyalty, and trust.

But the King who comes at Christmas
does not demand a throne.

He enters quietly.
He reigns in humility.
He comes not to rule over us,
but to dwell within us.

To find Him,
we do not look to power or applause — but to silence, simplicity, and love.

May we find His presence today, even in the places we least expect.

Lord Jesus, grant me the grace to love You more today than yesterday, and more tomorrow than today.

Amen.

Those Who Found Him

———————

On the night of Christ's birth,
only two kinds of people recognized Him:

The shepherds — the simple of heart,
who knew they knew nothing,
and were therefore open to wonder.

The wise men — the truly learned,
who had discovered that no matter how much they knew,
there was still mystery beyond their reach.

Both humility and wisdom bowed before Christ.

Pride did not kneel at Bethlehem.
Self-certainty did not travel to the manger.
The comfortable and complacent did not hear angels sing.

But those who were willing to be small,
or willing to keep searching, found Him.

Christmas invites us to return to that place:

the quiet of trust,
the honesty of need,
the reverent openness of the heart.

If we seek Him with humility,
we will find Him — just as they did.

May we find His presence today, even in the places we least expect.

*Lord Jesus, grant me the grace to love You more today than
yesterday, and more tomorrow than today. Amen.*

God Walked Where We Walk

The world is vast.
The stars are uncountable.
The universe overwhelms our smallness.

And yet — the greatest wonder is not in the heavens,
but in the truth that **God walked our earth.**

He breathed our air.
He worked with our hands.
He knew hunger, weariness, friendship, joy, and sorrow.

Other religions tell of humanity searching for God.
Christmas tells of **God searching for humanity.**

He came not in thunder or flame,
but with human feet on familiar ground.

The One who made the stars
walked beneath them.

The One who holds all things in existence
let Himself be held.

He did not come to overwhelm us — He came to be loved.

And He remains where hearts make room.

May we seek Him with reverence,
and welcome Him with tenderness.

The Footsteps of God

Sometimes we are reminded how small our earth is — a tiny speck in a vast universe. Yet its greatness lies not in its size, but in what happened upon it.

God walked here.

The One who scattered galaxies and shaped the stars chose to enter our world as a child. He breathed our air. He walked our roads. He touched our sorrow. He knew our hunger and our hope.

We are not merely searching for God.
God has searched for us.

He came not to dazzle us with power, but to draw near with love — to be held, to be known, to be welcomed.

And He still walks our earth — in every act of mercy,
in every humble offering,
in every heart that makes room for Him.

May we find His presence today, even in the places we least expect.

The Humility of God

To help us imagine the humility of the Incarnation,
Sheen asks us to picture what it would be like
to become a creature far below us,
to live among it,
to speak its limited language.

And then he tells us:

This is **only the faintest** comparison
to what God did for us.

The Child in the manger already bears within Him
the shadow of the Cross.
The humility that began in Bethlehem
is fulfilled on Calvary.

Love bends low — so low that nothing is beneath it.

That is the love that saves the world.

Do Not Settle for a "Safe" Jesus

———————

The world is comfortable speaking about Jesus as a teacher, a figure of history, a symbol of kindness — because such a Jesus asks little.

But the real Christ calls us to holiness.
He asks for our hearts, our decisions, our conversion.

A Christ who only inspires us but does not transform us
is not the Christ of Bethlehem.

He comes not to be admired — **but to be followed**.

Not to remain outside of us — **but to dwell within us**.

Let us not settle for the Christ of sentiment,
when the living Christ stands before us, calling us by name.

May we find His presence today, even in the places we least expect.

Lord Jesus, grant me the grace to love You more today than yesterday, and more tomorrow than today.

Amen.

Concluding Word

As we close these pages, may we not close our hearts. The mysteries of Advent and Christmas are not meant to be put away with the decorations, but to be lived in the quiet hours of every day.

Archbishop Fulton J. Sheen reminded us often that the crib, the Cross, and the altar are one continuous mystery of love. The wood of Bethlehem leads to the wood of Calvary, and from the sacrifice of the Cross flows the life of the Eucharist.

If Christ has been born anew in your soul during these days of prayer and reflection, then the purpose of this little book has been fulfilled. Let the Child of Bethlehem grow within you; let His light shine through you.

May Mary and Joseph, who welcomed Him first, teach us how to welcome Him always and may the Holy Spirit keep us watchful, joyful, and faithful until the day we see His face in glory.

"Christmas is not a day, but a state of the soul — when Christ is born anew in us."

— Archbishop Fulton J. Sheen

With every blessing in the Holy Child,

Allan J. Smith

About the Author

ALLAN SMITH is a Catholic evangelist, radio host, and spiritual director who has spent over a decade proclaiming the wisdom of Archbishop Fulton J. Sheen to audiences around the world. As the founder of Bishop Sheen Today, he has edited and published dozens of classic Sheen titles, including 'The Cries of Jesus from the Cross' and 'Lord, Teach Us to Pray'.

A passionate promoter of Eucharistic Reparation and devotion to the Holy Face of Jesus, Allan regularly speaks at parish missions, leads retreats, and hosts weekly radio broadcasts across Canada, the United States, Ireland, Australia and the Philippines. His work has helped reintroduce Sheen's powerful spiritual legacy to a new generation.

He lives in Canada with his family and continues his mission of calling souls to deeper intimacy with Christ through the example of saints like St. Thérèse of Lisieux and the timeless teachings of Fulton Sheen.

To learn more or to access free devotional resources,
visit our two websites at:

www.bishopsheentoday.com
www.holyfacemiracle.com

A Personal Invitation

Over the years, I have had the privilege of helping souls draw
closer to Christ through prayer, silence, and the timeless wisdom of
Archbishop Fulton J. Sheen.

Each of these books was written with a single desire:
to lead hearts more deeply into the mystery of Christ,
to encourage fidelity in prayer,
and to renew confidence in God's grace at work in ordinary life.

If this devotional has nourished your soul, you may find the
following works helpful companions on your spiritual journey:

The Sheen Mission Series

- *The Holy Face and the Little Way* — Volume I
- *Behold Your Mother* — Volume II
- *The Cross and the Last Words* — Volume III
- *Lord, Show Us Thy Face, and We Shall Be Saved* — Volume IV
- *The Sheen Mission Series: Collected Meditations*

Seasonal & Devotional Works

- *Advent and Christmas with Archbishop Fulton J. Sheen*
- *The Christmas Hour: Meditations for Advent, Christmas, and Epiphany*
- *The Twelve Days of Christmas and More: Mystery and Meaning*

Retreat & Formation

- *A Retreat with Archbishop Fulton J. Sheen: Five Paths of Reparation, Healing, and Holiness*

Living the Baptismal Call

- *Priest, Prophet & King: Living Your Baptismal Mission of Love and Service*
- *Priest, Prophet & King: Living Your Baptismal Mission in Everyday Life* (Abridged Edition)
- *Reparation, Healing and Holiness with the Help of Archbishop Fulton J. Sheen*

Each book may be read on its own, yet together they form a spiritual pathway — one that leads from the Heart of Christ, through the Cross, to a deeper life of trust, surrender, and hope.

May every page you read draw you closer to Our Lord. May prayer become more natural, faith more confident, and love more generous.

And may the Child of Bethlehem be born anew in your heart.

Come, Lord Jesus.

With every blessing,

Allan Smith

To learn more or to stay connected, please visit:
www.bishopsheentoday.com

Archbishop Fulton J. Sheen

† *Ora pro nobis* †

www.ingramcontent.com/pod-product-compliance
Lightning Source LLC
Chambersburg PA
CBHW060752050426
42449CB00008B/1371